A Machine Intelligence Primer for Clinicians

No Math or Programming Required

Alexander Scarlat MD

ISBN: 9781794256064
ISBN-13: 9781794256064

Dedicated to May, Adam & Dahlia

"Humans are like moths circling yesterday"

AI bot - Inspirobot.me

V2019.02.02

Cover image by Salvador Dali (1951):

Raphaelesque Head Exploding

Table of Contents

1. Introduction to Machine Intelligence

Machine Intelligence State of the Art in 2019

Near human or super-human performance:

- Image classification
- Speech recognition
- Handwriting transcription
- Machine translation
- Text-to-speech conversion
- Autonomous driving
- Digital assistants capable of conversation
- Go and chess games
- Music, picture, and text generation

Considering all the above — AI (artificial intelligence), ML (machine learning), machine intelligence, predictive analytics, computer vision, text and speech analysis — you may wonder:

How can a machine possibly learn ?!

As a physician with a degree in CS and curious about machine intelligence, I took the ML Stanford - Coursera course by Andrew Ng [1]. It was a painful, but at the same time an immensely pleasurable educational experience. Painful because of the non-trivial math involved. Immensely pleasurable because I've finally understood how a machine actually learns.

If you are a clinician who is interested in machine intelligence but short on math / programming skills or time, I will try to clarify in this book — what I have learned from my short personal journey in ML. You can check some of my machine intelligence projects at [2]. I promise that no math or programming are required for reading this book, which was initially published as a series of articles on HIStalk between October 2018 – January 2019 [3].

Rules-Based Systems

The ancient predecessors of ML are the rules-based systems. They are easy to explain to humans:

- IF the blood pressure is normal +/- 25 percent
- AND the heart rate is normal and up to normal + 27 percent
- AND the urinary output is normal or down to normal – 43 percent
- AND / OR etc.
- THEN consider septic shock as part of the differential diagnosis.

The problem with these systems is that they are time-consuming, error-prone, difficult and expensive to build and test, and do not perform well in real life. Rules-based systems also do not adapt to new situations that the model has never seen.

Even when rules-based systems predict something, it is based on a human-derived rule, on a human's (limited?) understanding of the problem and how well that human represented the restrictions in the rules-based system.

One can argue about the statistical validation that is behind each and every parameter in the above short example rule. You can imagine what will happen with a truly big, complex system with thousands or millions of rules.

Rules-based systems are founded on a delicate and very brittle process that doesn't scale well to complex medical problems.

ML Definitions

Two definitions of machine learning are widely used:

1. *"The field of study that gives computers the ability to learn without being explicitly programmed."* (Arthur Samuel).

2. *"A computer program is said to learn from experience (E) with respect to some class of tasks (T) and performance measure (P) — IF its performance at tasks in T, as measured by P, improves with experience E."* (Tom Mitchell).

Rules-based systems, therefore are by definition not a ML model. They are explicitly programmed according to some fixed, hard-wired set of finite rules.

With any model, ML or not ML, or any other common sense approach to a task, one must measure the model performance. How good are the model predictions when compared to real life? The distance between the model predictions and the real-life data is being measured with a metric, such as accuracy or mean-squared error.

A true ML model must learn with each and every new experience and improve its performance with each learning step while using an optimization and loss function to calibrate its own model weights. Monitoring and fine-tuning the learning process is an important part of training a ML algorithm.

What's the Difference Between ML and Statistics?

While ML and statistics share a similar background and use similar terms and basic methods like accuracy, precision, recall, etc., there is a heated debate about the differences between the two. The best answer I found is the one in Francois Chollet's excellent book - Deep Learning with Python [4].

Imagine Data going into a black box, which uses Rules (classical statistical programming) and then predicts Answers:

One provides Statistics, the Data, and the Rules. Statistics will predict the Answers.

ML takes a different approach:

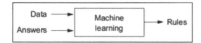

One provides ML, the Data, and the Answers. ML will return the Rules learned.

The last figure depicts only the training / learning phase of ML known as FIT – the model fits to the experiences learned – while learning the Rules. Then one can use these machine learned Rules with new Data, never seen by the model before, to PREDICT Answers.

Fit / Predict are the basics of a ML model life cycle: the model learns (or train / fit) and then it predicts on new Data.

Why is ML Better than Traditional Statistics for Some Tasks?

There are numerous examples where there are no statistical models available: on-line multi-lingual translation, voice recognition, or identifying melanoma in a series of photos better than a group of dermatologists. All are ML-based models, with some theoretical foundations in Statistics.

ML has a higher capacity to represent complex, multi-dimensional problems. A model, be it statistical or ML, has inherent, limited, problem-representation capabilities. Think about predicting inpatient mortality based on only one parameter, such as age. Such a model will quickly achieve a certain performance ceiling it cannot possibly overpass, as it is limited in its capabilities to represent the true complexity involved in this type of prediction. The mortality prediction problem is much more complicated than considering only age.

On the other hand, a model that takes into consideration 10,000 parameters when predicting mortality (diagnosis at admission, procedures, lab, imaging, pathology results, medications, consultations, etc.) has a theoretically much higher capacity to better represent the problem complexity, the numerous interrelations that may exist within the data, non-linear, complex relation and such. ML deals with multivariate, multi-dimensional complex issues better than statistics.

ML model predictions are not bound by the human understanding of a problem or the human decision to use a specific model in a specific situation. One can test 20 ML models with thousands of dimensions each on the same problem and pick the top five to create an ensemble of models. Using this architecture allows several mediocre-performing models to achieve a genius level just by combining their individual, non-stellar predictions. While it will be difficult for a human to understand the reasoning of such an ensemble of models, it may still outperform and beat humans by a large margin. Statistics was never meant to deal with this kind of challenges.

Statistical models do not scale well to the billions of rows of data currently available and used for analysis.

Statistical models can't work when there are no Rules. ML models can – it's called unsupervised learning. For example, segment a patient population into five groups. Which groups, you may ask? What are their specifications (a.k.a. Rules)? ML magic: even as we don't know the specs of these five groups, an algorithm can still segment the patient population and then tell us about these five groups' specs.

Why the Recent Increased Interest in AI/ML?

The recent increased interest in AI/ML is attributed to several factors:

- Improved algorithms derived from the last decade progress in the math foundations of ML
- Better hardware, specifically designed for ML needs, based on the video gaming industry GPU (graphic processor unit)
- Huge quantity of data available as a playground for nascent data scientists
- Capability to transfer learning and reuse models trained by others for different purposes
- Most importantly, having all the above as free, open source while being supported by a great users' community

References:

1. https://www.coursera.org/learn/machine-learning/
2. https://scarlatsquared.wordpress.com/
3. https://histalk2.com/category/ml-primer/
4. Deep Learning with Python by Francois Chollet

2. Supervised Learning

To recap from the previous chapter, the difference between traditional statistical models and ML models in their approach to a problem:

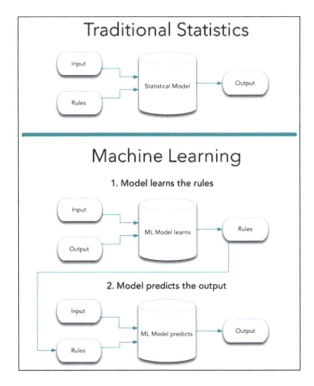

We feed Statistics an input and some rules and it provides back an output.

With a ML model we have two steps:

1. We feed ML an input and the output and the ML model learns the rules. This learning phase is also called training or model fit.
2. Then ML uses these rules to predict the output.

In an increasing number of fields we realize that these - rules learned by the machine - are much better than the rules we humans can come up with.

Supervised vs. Unsupervised Learning

With the above in mind - the difference between supervised and unsupervised is simple:

Supervised learning - we do know the labels of each input instance. We have the Output (eg: Discharged home, $85,300 costs to patient, 12 days ICU, 18% chance of being readmitted within 30 days). Regression to a continuous variable (number) and Classification to two or more classes are the main sub categories of Supervised learning.

Unsupervised learning - we do not have the output. Actually we may have no idea how the Output looks like. Note that in this case there's no teacher (in the form of Output) and no rules around to tell the

ML model what's correct and what's not during learning. Clustering, Anomaly Detection and Primary Component Analysis are the main sub categories of Unsupervised learning.

Other - models working in parallel, one on top of another in ensembles, some models supervising other models which in turn are unsupervised, some of these models getting into a "generative adversarial relationship" with other models (not my terminology) ... a veritable zoo, an exciting ecosystem of ML model architectures that is growing fast, as people experiment with new ideas and existing tools.

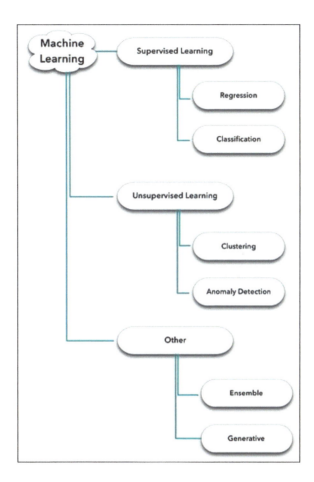

Supervised Learning - Regression
With regression problems the Output is continuous - a number like the LOS (number of hours or days the patient was in hospital) or the number of days in ICU, Costs to patient, Days till next readmission, etc. It is also called regression to continuous arbitrary values.
Let's take a quick look at the input (a thorough discussion about how to properly feed data to a baby ML model will follow in one of the next chapters).
At this stage, think about the input as a table - rows are samples and columns are features.
If we have a single column or feature - Age - and the output label is LOS - then it may be either a Linear regression or a Polynomial (non-linear) regression:

Linear Regression
Reusing Tom Mitchell definition of a machine learning algorithm:
" A computer program is said to learn from Experience (E) with respect to some class of tasks (T) and performance (P) - IF its performance at tasks in T, as measure by P, improves with experience (E)"

The *Task* is to find the best straight line between the scatters points below - LOS vs. Age - so that in turn, can be used later for prediction of new instances
The *Experience* are all the X and Y data points we have
The *Performance* will be measured as the distance between the model prediction and the real value.

X axis is Age, Y is LOS (disregard the scale for the sake of discussion). Monitoring the model learning process, we can see how it approaches the best line with the given data (X and Y) while going thru an iterative process:

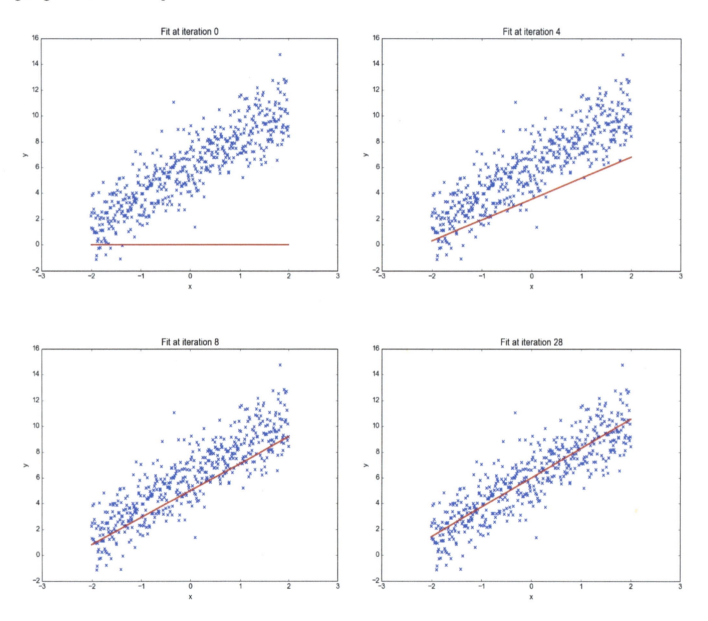

From Linear Regression the Easier Way by Sagar Sharma [1].

Polynomial (Non-linear) regression

What happens when the relationship between our single variable Age and output LOS is not linear ?
The *Task* is to find the best line - obviously not a straight line - to describe the (non-linear) polynomial relationship between X (Age) and Y (LOS):

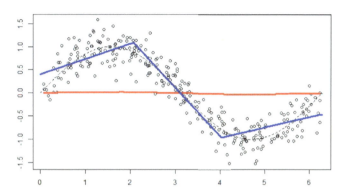

The *Experience* and *Performance* stay the same as in the previous example.
As above, monitoring the model learning process as it approximates the data (*Experience*) during the fit process (each figure represents approx. 20 iterations):

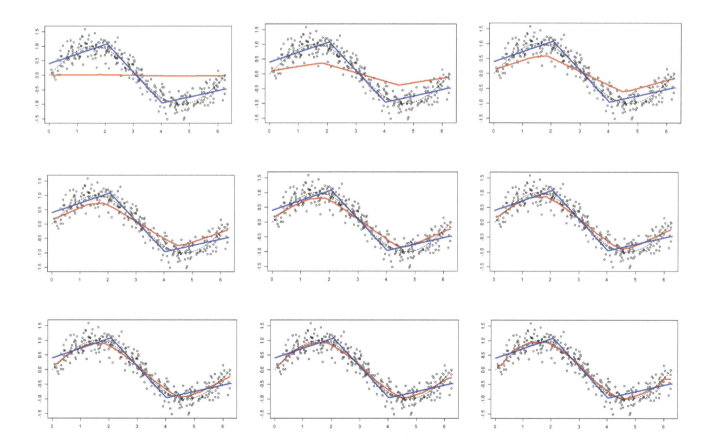

From R-english Freakonometrics by Arthur Carpentier [2]

Life is a bit more complicated than one feature (Age) when predicting LOS, so we'd like to see what happens with 2 features - Age and BMI - how they contribute to LOS, when taken together.

The *Task* is to predict the Z axis (vertical) with a set of X and Y (horizontal plane).
The *Experience* we feed the model now has 2 features: Age and BMI. The output stays the same: LOS.
The *Performance* is measured as above.

Find the following peaks chart - a function - similar to the linear line or the polynomial line we found above. This time the function defines the input as a plane (Age on X and BMI on Y) and the output LOS on Z axis. Knowing a specific Age as X and BMI as Y and using such a function / peaks 3D chart - one can predict LOS as Z:

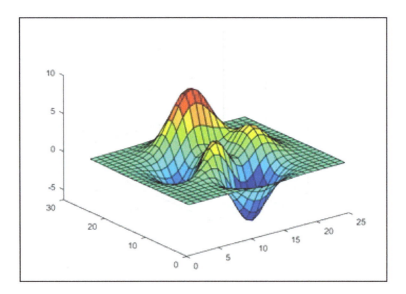

A peaks chart usually has a contour chart accompanying, visualizing the relationships between X, Y and Z (note that besides X and Y - color is considered a dimension too - Z - on a contour chart). The contour chart of the 3D chart above:

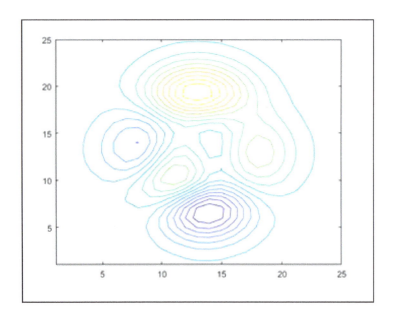

From MathWorks manual [3]

How does a 4D problem may look like ?
If we add the time as another dimension to a 3D like the one above, it becomes a 4D chart (disregard the axes and title):

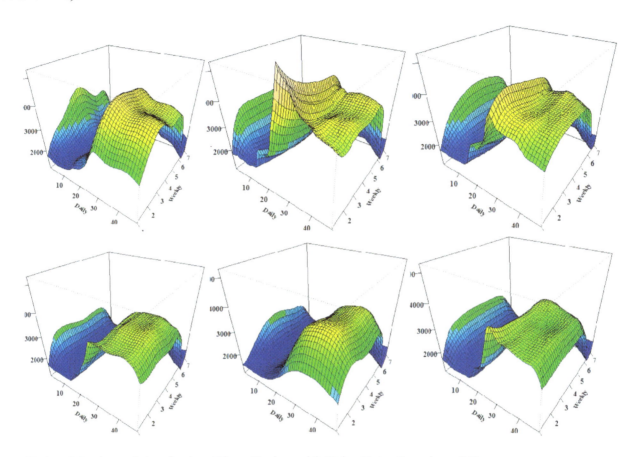

From Doing Magic and Analyzing Time Series with R by Peter Laurinec [4]

Supervised Learning - Classification
When the output is discrete, not continuous - then the problem is one of classification. Please note ! Classification problems are also called - Logistic Regression - that's a misnomer and just causes confusion.

- **Binary classification** eg: Dead / Live
- **Multi-class classification** eg: Discharged home / Transferred to another facility / Discharged to Nursing facility / Died / etc.

One can take a regression problem like LOS and make it a classification problem using several buckets or classes:

- LOS between 0 and 4 days
- LOS between 5 and 8 days
- LOS between 9 and 11 days
- LOS greater than 12 days, etc.

Binary Classification with two variables

Task: find the best straight line that separates between the blue and red dots - the decision boundary between the two classes

Experience: given the input of the X and Y coordinate of each dot - predict the output as the color of the dot: blue or red

Performance: Accuracy of the prediction. Note that just by chance, no ML involved - the accuracy of guessing is expected to be around 50% in this of type of binary classification, as the blue and the red classes are well balanced.

Visualizing the data - it seems there may be a relatively straight line to separate the dots. The model learning iteratively the best separating straight line. This model is linearly constrained when searching for a decision boundary:

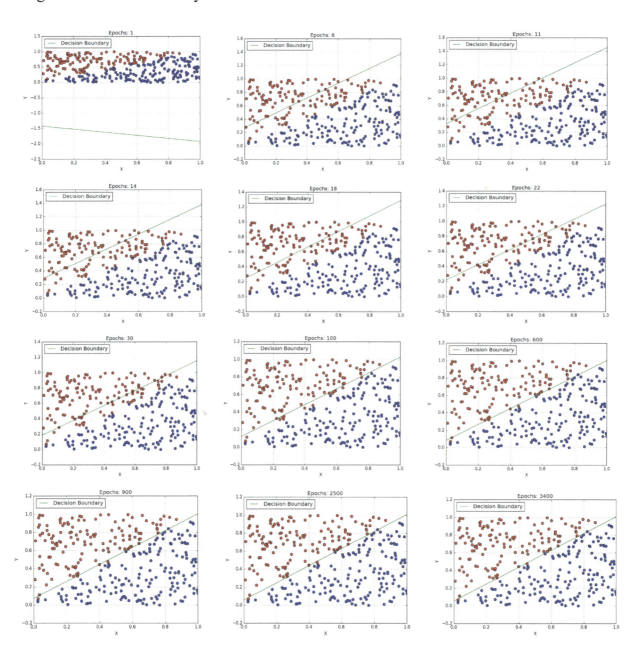

From Classification by Davi Frossard [5]

Binary Classification with a Non-Linear Separation

A bit more complex dots separation exercise, when the separation line is obviously non-linear. The *Task*, *Experience* and *Performance* remain the same:

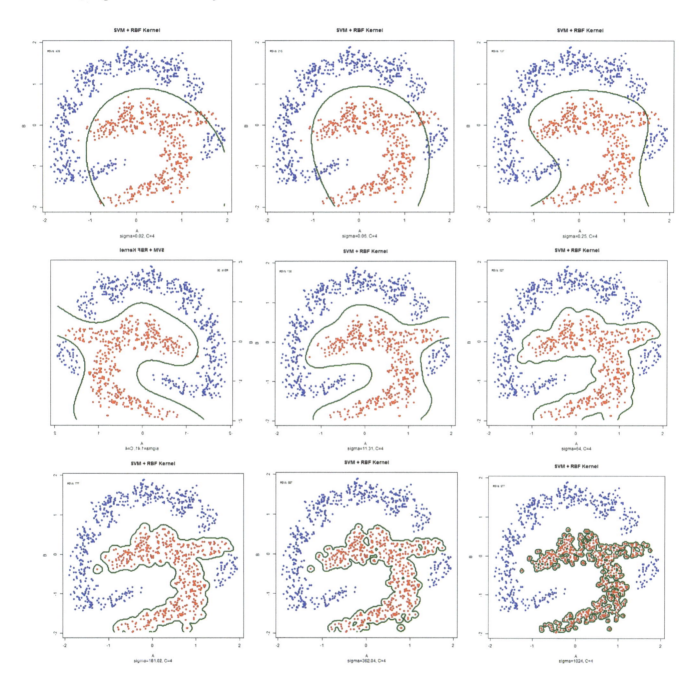

The ML model learning the best decision boundary, while not being constrained to a linear solution: From gfycat [6]

Multi-class Classification

Multi-class classification is actually an extension of the simple binary classification. It's called the "One-vs-All" technique. Consider 3 groups: A, B and C. If we know how to do a Binary classification (see above) - then we can calculate probabilities for:

- A vs. all the others (B and C)
- B vs. all the others (A and C)
- C vs. all the others (A and B)

More about Classification models in the next chapters.

Binary Classification with 3 variables

While the last example had 2 variables (X and Y) with one output (color of the dot), the next one has 3 input variables (X, Y and Z) and the same output: color of the dot.
Task: find the best HYPERPLANE shape (a.k.a. rules / function) to separate between the blue and red dots
Experience has now 3 input variables (X, Y and Z) and one output label: the dot color
Performance remains the same as before.

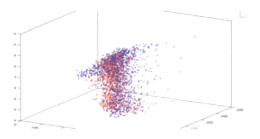

From Ammon Washburn - Data Scientist [7]

So how can we visualize a problem with 5,000 dimensions ?
Unfortunately, we cannot visualize more than 4-5 dimensions. The above 4D chart (3D plus time) on a map with multiple locations - charts running in parallel, over time - I guess that would be considered a 5D visualization - having the geo location as the fifth dimension. One can imagine how difficult it would be to actually visualize, absorb and digest the information and just monitor such a (limited) 5D problem for a couple of days.

Alas, if it's difficult for us to visualize and monitor a 5D problem - how can we expect to learn from each and every experience of such a complex system and improve our performance, in real-time on a prediction task ?
How about a problem with 10,000 features, the task of predicting one out of 467 DRG classifications for a specific patient, with an error less than 8% ?

In this book we'll tackle problems with many features and many dimensions, while visualizing additional monitors - the ML learning curves - which in my opinion are as beautiful and informative as the charts above, even as they are only 2D.

Other ML Architectures

On an artsy note, as it is related to the third group of ML models - Other - in my chart above. Models that are not purely supervised or unsupervised.

In 2015, Gatys et al. published a paper on a model that separates style from content in a painting [8]. The generative model learns an artist style and then predicts the style effects learned, on any arbitrary image. The left upper corner is an image in Europe and then each cell is the same image rendered in one of several famous painters' styles:

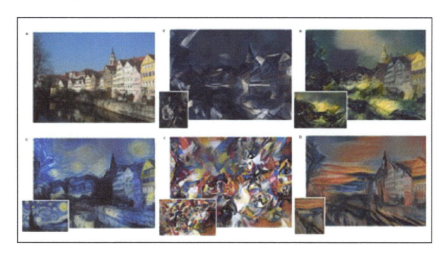

Scoff you may, but in October 2018 the first piece of art generated by AI fetched $432,500 at Christie's [9].

Generative ML models have been trained to generate text in a Shakespearean style or the Bible style - by feeding ML models with all Shakespeare or the whole Bible text. Recently humans started feeding ML models the actual Linux and Python programming languages (the relevant documentation, manuals, Q&A forums, etc.). As expected, the machines started writing computer code on their own. The computer software written by machines cannot be compiled nor executed and it will not actually run. Yet ...

It is an intriguing, philosophical, recursive thought - computers writing their own software…

References:

1. https://towardsdatascience.com/linear-regression-the-easier-way-6f941aa471ea
2. https://freakonometrics.hypotheses.org/tag/r-english
3. https://nl.mathworks.com/help/matlab/examples/creating-3-d-plots_ja_JP.html?s_tid=gn_loc_drop
4. https://www.r-bloggers.com/doing-magic-and-analyzing-seasonal-time-series-with-gam-generalized-additive-model-in-r/
5. https://www.cs.toronto.edu/~frossard/post/classification/
6. https://gfycat.com/gifs/detail/sentimentalthickbullfrog
7. http://math.arizona.edu/~wammonj/research/SVMVisuals.html
8. https://arxiv.org/abs/1508.06576
9. https://news.artnet.com/market/first-ever-artificial-intelligence-portrait-painting-sells-at-christies-1379902

3. Unsupervised Learning

In the previous chapter, we've defined unsupervised machine learning as the type of algorithm used to draw inferences from input data without having a clue about the output expected. There are no labels such as patient outcome, diagnosis, LOS, etc. to provide a feedback mechanism during the model training process.

In this chapter, we'll focus on the two most common models of unsupervised learning: clustering and anomaly detection.

Unsupervised Clustering

As a motivating factor, consider the following image from Wikipedia [1]:

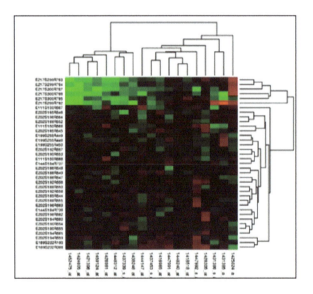

The above is a heat map that details the influence of a set of parameters on the expression (production) of a set of genes. Red means increased expression and green means reduced expression. A clustering model has organized the information in a heat map plus the hierarchical clustering on top and on the right sides of the diagram above.

There are two types of clustering models:

- Models that need to be told a priori the number of groups / clusters we're looking for
- Models that will find the optimal number of clusters

Consider a simple dataset:

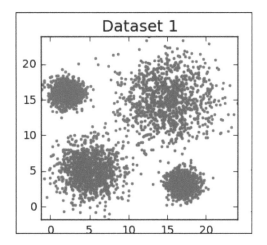

Task: identify the four clusters in Dataset1.

Experience: sets of X and Y and the number of groups (four in the above example).

Performance metric: total sum of the squared distances of each point in a cluster from its centroid (the center of the cluster) location.

The model initializes four centroids, usually at a random location. The centroids are then moved according to a cost function that the model tries to minimize at each iteration. The cost function is the total sum of the squared distance of each point in the cluster from its centroid. The process is repeated iteratively until there is little or no improvement in the cost function.

In the figures below you can see how the centroids – white X's – are moving towards the centers of their clusters in parallel to the decreasing cost function on the right:

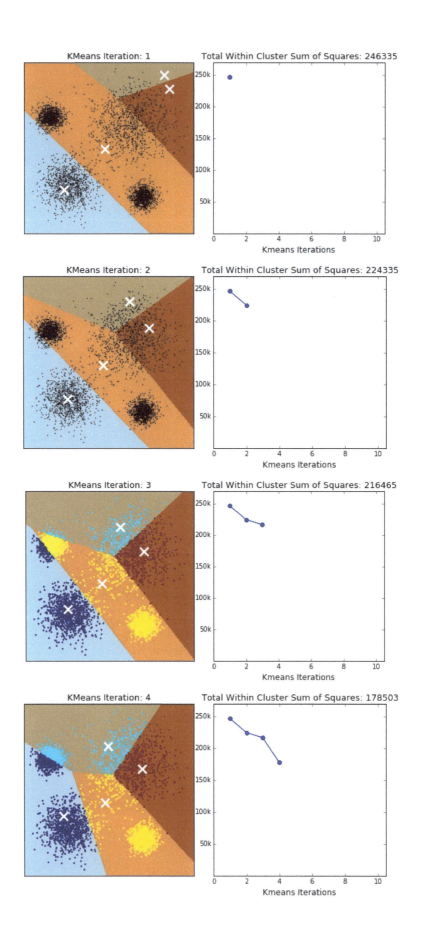

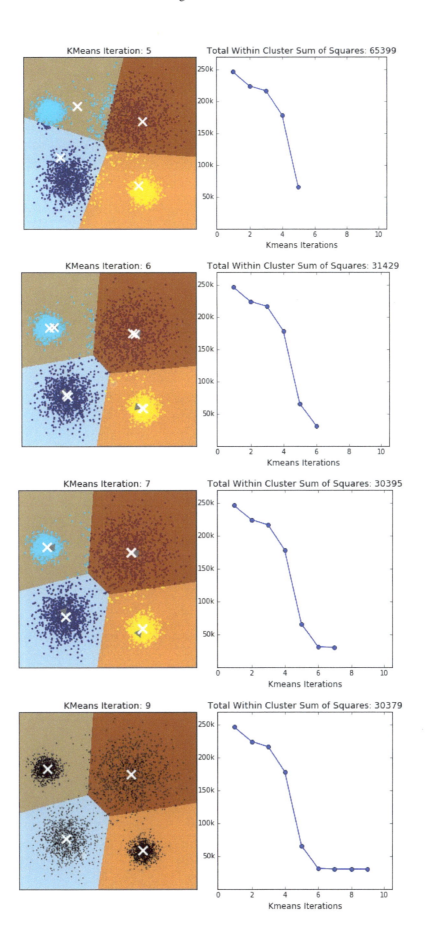

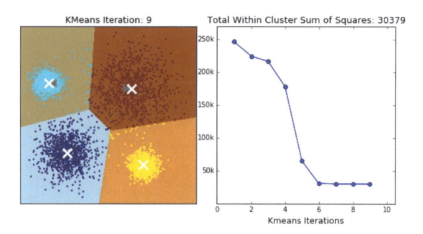

While doing great on Dataset1, the same model fails miserably on Dataset2, so pick your clustering ML model wisely by exposing the model to diverse experiences / datasets:

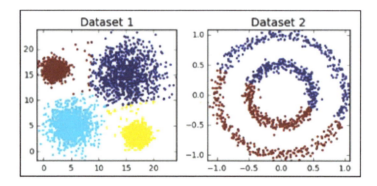

Clustering models that don't need to know a priori the number of centroids (groups) will have the following problem definition:

Task: identify the clusters in Dataset1 with the lowest cost function.
Experience: sets of X and Y (there are NO number of groups / centroids).
Performance metric: same as above.

The model below initializes randomly many centroids and then works through an algorithm that tells it how to consolidate together other neighboring centroids to reduce the number of groups to the overall lowest cost function:

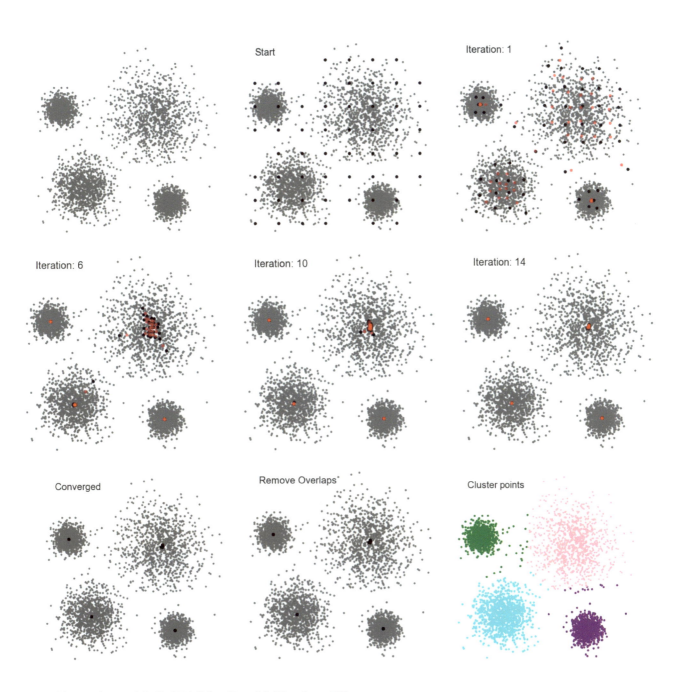

From "Clustering with SciKit" by David Sheehan [2]

3D Clustering

While the above example had as input two dimensions (features) X and Y, the following gene expression in a population has three dimensions: X, Y, and Z. The mission definition for such a clustering ML model is the same as above, except the input has now three features: X, Y, and Z:

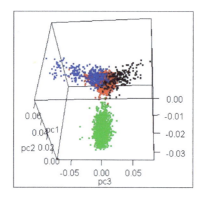

Unsupervised Anomaly Detection

As a motivating factor, consider the new criteria for early identification of patients at risk for sepsis or septic shock, qSOFA 2018 [3]. The three main rules of qSOFA:

1. Glasgow Coma Scale (GCS) < 15
2. Respiratory rate (RR) >= 22
3. Systolic blood pressure (BP) <=100 mmHg

Let's focus on two parameters, RR and BP, and a patient who presents with:
RR = 21/minute and systolic BP = 102 mmHg

A rule-based engine with only two rules will miss this patient, as it doesn't sound the alarm per the above qSOFA definition. Not if the rule was written with the logical AND and not it had the logical OR between the conditions. Can a ML model do better? Would you define the above two parameters, when taken together, as an anomaly ?
Before explaining how a machine can detect anomalies unsupervised by humans, a quick reminder from Gauss (born 1777) about his eponymous distribution.

One-Variable Gaussian Distribution

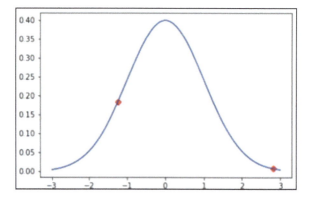

You may remember from statistics that the above bell-shaped normal Gaussian distribution can accurately describe many phenomena around us. The mean on the above X axis is zero and then there are several standard deviations around the mean (from -3 to +3). The Y axis defines the probability of X. Each point on the chart has a probability of occurrence: the red dot on the right can be defined as an anomaly with a probability of ~ 1 percent. The dot on the left side has a probability of ~ 18 percent, so most probably it's not an anomaly.

The sum (integral) of a Gaussian probability distribution is one, or 100 percent. Thus, even an event right on top of our chart has a probability of only 40 percent. Given a point on the X axis and using the Gaussian distribution, we can easily predict the probability of that event happening.

Two-Variable Gaussian Distribution

Back to the patient that exhibits RR = 21 and BP=102 and the decision whether this patient is in for a septic shock adventure or not. There are two variables: X and Y, and a new problem definition:

Task: automatically identify instances as anomalies if they are beyond a given threshold. Let's set the anomaly threshold at three percent.
Experience: sets of X and Y and the threshold to be considered an anomaly (three percent).
Performance metric: number of correct vs. incorrect classifications with a test set, with known anomalies (more about unbalanced classes in next chapters).

The following 3D peaks chart has X (RR), Y (BP), and the Gaussian probability as Z axis. Each point on the X-Y plane has a probability associated with it on the Z axis. Usually a peaks chart has an accompanying contour map in which the 3D is flattened to 2D, with the color still expressing the probability.

Note the elongated, oblong shape of both the peaks chart and the contour map underneath it. This is the crucial fact: the shape of the Gaussian distribution of X and Y is not a circle (which we may have naively assumed), it's elliptical. On the peaks chart, there is a red dot with its corresponding red dot on the contour map below:

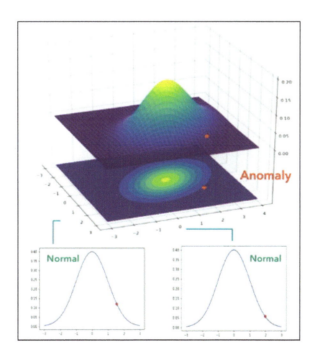

The elliptic shape of our probability distribution of X and Y helps visualizing the following:

- Each parameter, when considered separately on its own probability distribution, is within its normal limits.
- Both parameters, when taken together, are definitely abnormal, an anomaly with a probability of ~ 0.8 percent (0.008 on the Z axis), much smaller than the three percent threshold wee set above.

Unsupervised anomaly detection should be considered when:

- The number of normal instances is much larger than the number of anomalies. We just don't have enough samples of labeled anomalies to use with a supervised model.
- There may be unforeseen instances and combinations of parameters that when considered together are abnormal. Remember that a supervised model cannot predict or detect instances never seen during training. Unsupervised anomaly detection models can deal with the unforeseen circumstances by using a function from the 1800s.

Scale the above two-parameter model to one that considers hundreds to thousands of patient parameters, together and at the same time, and you have an unsupervised anomaly detection ML model to prevent patients deterioration, while being monitored in a clinical environment.

The fascinating part about ML algorithms is that we can easily scale a model to thousands of dimensions while having, at the same time, a severe human limitation to visualize more than 5D (see previous chapter on how a 4D / 5D problem may look).

References:
1. https://en.wikipedia.org/wiki/Gene_expression_profiling
2. https://dashee87.github.io/data%20science/general/Clustering-with-Scikit-with-GIFs/
3. https://www.mdcalc.com/qsofa-quick-sofa-score-sepsis

4. How to Properly Feed Data to a ML Model

While in the previous chapters I've tried to give you an idea about what AI / ML models can do for us, in this chapter, I'll sketch what we must do for the machines before asking them to perform magic. Specifically, the data preparation before it can be fed into a ML model.

For the moment, assume the raw data is arranged in a table with samples as rows and features as columns. These raw features / columns may contain free text; categorical text; discrete data such as ethnicity; integers like heart rate, floating point numbers like 12.58 as well as ICD, DRG, CPT codes; images; voice recordings; videos; waveforms, etc.

What are the dietary restrictions of an artificial intelligence agent? ML models love their diet to consist of only floating point numbers, preferably small values, centered and scaled /normalized around their means +/- their standard deviations.

No Relational Data

If we have a relational database management system (RDBMS), we must first flatten the one-to-many relationships and summarize them, so one sample or instance fed into the model is truly a good representative summary of that instance. For example, one patient may have many hemoglobin lab results, so we need to decide what to feed the ML model — the minimum Hb, maximum, Hb averaged daily, only abnormal Hb results, number of abnormal results per day?

No Missing Values

There can be no missing values, as it is similar to swallowing air while eating. 0 and n/a are not considered missing values. Null is definitely a missing value. The most common methods of imputing missing values are:

- Numbers – the mean, median, 0, etc.
- Categorical data – the most frequent value, n/a or 0

No Text

We all know by now that the genetic code is made of raw text with only four letters (A,C,T,G). Before you run to feed your ML model some raw DNA data and ask it questions about the meaning of life, remember that one cannot feed a ML model raw text. Not unless you want to see an AI entity burp and barf.

There are various methods to transform words or characters into numbers. All of them start with a process of tokenization, in which a larger unit of language is broken into smaller tokens. Usually it suffices to break a document into words and stop there:

- Document into sentences.
- Sentence into words.
- Sentence into n-grams, word structures that try to maintain the same semantic meaning (three-word n-grams will assume that chronic atrial fibrillation, atrial chronic fibrillation, fibrillation atrial chronic are all the same concept).

- Words into characters.

Once the text is tokenized, there are two main approaches of text-to-numbers transformations so text will become more palatable to the ML model:

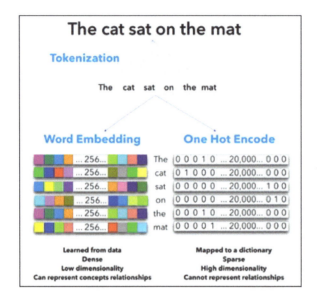

One Hot Encode (right side of the above figure)

Using a dictionary of the 20,000 most commonly used words in the English language, we create a large table with 20,000 columns. Each word becomes a row of 20,000 columns. The word "cat" in the above figure is encoded as: 0,1,0,0,…. 20,000 columns, all 0's except one column with 1. One Hot Encoder – as only one column gets the 1, all the others get 0.

This a widely used, simple transformation which has several limitations:

- The table created will be mostly sparse, as most of the values will be 0 across a row. Sparse tables with high dimensionality (20,000) have their own issues, which may cause a severe indigestion to a ML model, named the Curse of Dimensionality (see below).
- In addition, one cannot represent the order of the words in a sentence with a One Hot Encoder.

In many cases, such as sentiment analysis of a document, it seems the order of the words doesn't really matter. Words like "superb," "perfectly" vs. "awful," "horrible" pretty much give away the document sentiment, disregarding where exactly in the document they actually appear:

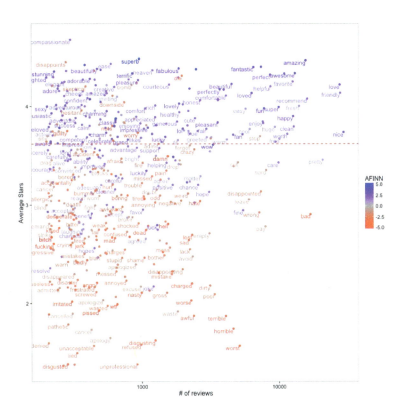

From "Does sentiment analysis work? A tidy analysis of Yelp reviews" by David Robinson [1].

On the other hand, one can think about a medical document in which a term is negated, such as "no signs of meningitis." In a model where the order of the words is not important, one can foresee a problem with the algorithm not truly understanding the meaning of the negation at the beginning of the sentence.

The semantic relationship between the words mother-father, king-queen, France-Paris, and Starbucks-coffee will be missed by such an encoding process.

Plurals such as child-children will be missed by the One Hot Encoder and will be considered as unrelated terms.

Word Embedding / Vectorization

A different approach is to encode words into multi-dimensional arrays of floating point numbers (tensors) that are either learned on the fly for a specific job or using an existing pre-trained model such as word2vec, which is offered by Google and trained mostly on Google news.

Basically a ML model will try to figure the best word vectors — as related to a specific context — and then encode the data to tensors (numbers) in many dimensions so another model may use it down the pipeline.

This approach does not use a fixed dictionary with the top 20,000 most-used words in the English language. It will learn the vectors from the specific context of the documents being fed and create its own multi-dimensional tensors "dictionary."

An Argentinian start-up generates legal papers without lawyers and suggests a ruling, which in 33 out of 33 cases has been accepted by a human judge [2].

Word vectorization is context sensitive. A great set of vectorized legal words (like the Argentinian start-up may have used) will fail when presented with medical terms and vice versa.

In the figure above, I've used many colors, instead of 0 and 1, in each cell of the word embedding example to give an idea about 256 dimensions and their capability to store information in a much denser format. Please do not try to feed colors directly to a ML model as it may void your warranty.

Consider an example where words are vectors in two dimensions (not 256). Each word is an arrow starting at 0,0 and ending on some X,Y coordinates:

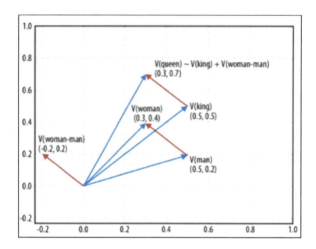

From Deep Learning Cookbook by Douwe Osinga [3].

The interesting part about words as vectors is that we can now visualize, in a limited 2D space, how the conceptual distance between the terms man-woman is being translated by the word vectorization algorithm into a physical geometrical distance, which is quite similar to the distance between the terms king-queen. If in only two dimensions the algorithm can generalize from man-woman to king-queen, what can it learn about more complex semantic relationships and hundreds of dimensions?
We can ask such a ML model interesting questions and get answers that are already beyond human level performance:

- Q: Paris is to France as Berlin is to? A: Germany.
- Q: Starbucks is to coffee as Apple is to? A: IPhone.
- Q: What are the capitals of all the European countries? A: UK-London, France-Paris, Romania-Bucharest, etc.
- Q: What are the three products IBM is most related to? A: DB2, WebSphere Portal, Tamino_XML_Server.
- The above are real examples using a a model trained on Google news.
- One can train a ML model with relevant vectorized medical text and see if it can answer questions like:
- Q: Acute pulmonary edema is to CHF as ketoacidosis is to? A: diabetes.
- Q: What are the three complications a cochlear implant is related to? A: flap necrosis, improper electrode placement, facial nerve problems.
- Q: Who are the two most experienced surgeons in my home town for a TKR? A: Jekyll, Hyde.

Word vectorization allows other ML models to deal with text (as tensors) — models that do care about the order of the words, such as algorithms that deal with time sequences.

Discrete Categories

Consider a drop-down with the following mutually exclusive drugs:

1. Viadur
2. Viagra
3. Vibramycin
4. Vicodin

As the above text seems already encoded (eg. Vicodin=4), you may be tempted to eliminate the text and leave the numbers as the encoded values for these drugs. That's not a good idea. The algorithm will erroneously deduce there is a conceptual similarity between the above drugs just because of their similar range of numbers. After all, two and three are really close from a machine's perspective, especially if it is a 20,000-drug list.

The list of drugs being ordered alphabetically by their brand names doesn't imply there is any conceptual or pharmacological relationship between Viagra and Vibramycin.

Mutually exclusive categories are transformed to numbers with the One Hot Encoder technique detailed above. The result will be a table with the columns: Viadur, Viagra, Vibramycin, Viocodin (similar to the words tokenized above: "the," "cat," etc.) Each instance (row) will have one and only one of the above columns encoded with a 1, while all the others will be encoded to 0. In this arrangement, the algorithm is not induced into error and the model will not find conceptual relationships where there are none.

Normalization

When an algorithm is comparing numerical values such as creatinine=3.8, age=1, heparin=5,000, the ML model will give a disproportionate importance and incorrect interpretation to the heparin parameter, just because heparin has a high raw value when compared to all the other numbers.
One of the most common solutions is to normalize each column:

- Calculate the mean and standard deviation
- Replace the raw values with the new normalized ones

When normalized, the algorithm will correctly interpret the creatinine and the age of the patient to be the important, deviant from the average kind of features in this sample, while the heparin will be regarded as normal.

Curse of Dimensionality

If you have a table with 10,000 features (columns), you may think that's great as it is feature-rich. But if this table has fewer than 10,000 samples (examples), you should expect ML models that would vehemently refuse to digest your data set or just produce really weird outputs.

This is called the curse of dimensionality. As the number of dimensions increases, the "volume" of the hyperspace created increases much faster, to a point where the data available becomes sparse. That interferes with achieving any statistical significance on any metric and will also prevent a ML model from finding clusters since the data is too sparse.

Preferably the number of samples should be at least three orders of magnitude larger than the number of features. A 10,000-column table had be better garnished by at least 10,000 rows (samples).

Tensors

After all the effort invested in the data preparation above, what kind of tensors can we offer now as food for thought to a machine ?

- 2D – table: samples, features
- 3D – time sequences: samples, features, time
- 4D – images: samples, height, width, RGB (color)
- 5D – videos: samples, frames, height, width, RGB (color)

Note that samples is the first dimension in all cases.

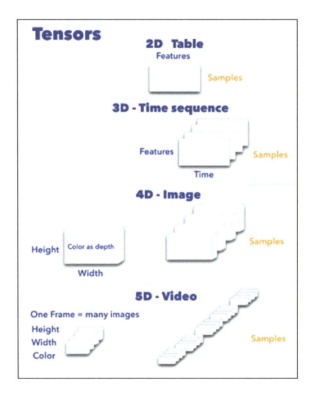

Hopefully this chapter will cause no indigestion to any human or artificial entity.

References:

1. http://varianceexplained.org/r/yelp-sentiment/
2. https://www.bloomberg.com/news/articles/2018-10-26/this-ai-startup-generates-legal-papers-without-lawyers-and-suggests-a-ruling?srnd=businessweek-v2
3. https://www.amazon.com/Deep-Learning-Cookbook-Practical-Recipes-ebook/dp/B07DK1ZZXT?keywords=douwe+osinga&qid=1540440172&s=Books&sr=1-1-fkmrnull&ref=sr_1_fkmrnull_1

5. How Does a Machine Actually Learn?

Most ML models will have the following components:

- **Weights** – units that contain the model parameters and are modified with each new learning experience. a.k.a train epoch.
- **Metric** – a measure (accuracy, mean square error) of the distance between the model prediction and the true value of that epoch.
- **Loss or Cost Function** – used to update the weights with each train epoch according to the calculated metric.
- **Optimizer** – algorithm overseeing the loss function so the model will find the global minimum in a reasonable time frame, basically preventing the model from wondering all over the loss function hyperspace.

The learning process or model training is done in epochs. With each epoch, the model is exposed to a batch of samples. Each epoch has two steps:

- **Forward propagation of the input.** The input features undergo math calculations with all the model weights and the model predicts an output.
- **Back propagation of the errors**. The model prediction is compared to the real output. This metric is used by the loss function and its master – the optimizer algorithm – to update all the weights according to the last epoch performance.

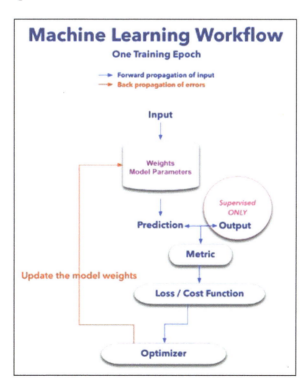

Consider a model, in this case a neural network (NN) that tries to predict LOS using two features: age and BMI. We have a table with 100 samples / instances / rows and three columns: age, BMI, and LOS.

Task: using age and BMI, predict the LOS
Input: age and BMI
Output: LOS
Performance: mean square error (MSE), the squared difference between predicted and true value of LOS.

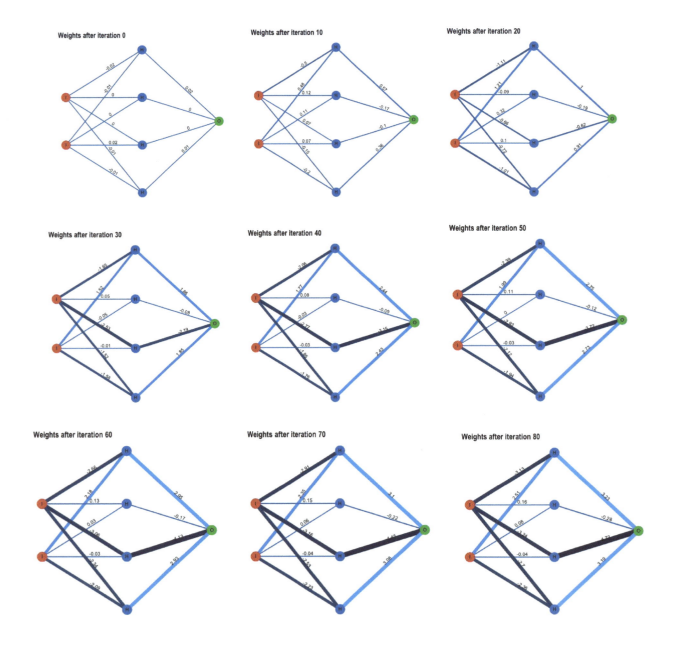

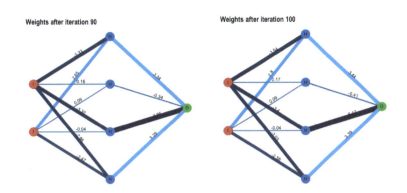

Forward Propagation of the Input

Input is being fed one batch at a time. In our example, let's assume the batch size is equal to one sample (instance). In the above case, one instance enters the model at the two left red dots: one for age and one for BMI (I stands for Input). The model weights are initialized as very small, random numbers near zero.

All the input features of one instance interact simultaneously through a complex mathematical transformation with all the model parameters (weights are denoted with H from hidden). These interactions are then summarized as the model LOS prediction at the rightmost green dot – output.

Note the numbers on the diagram above and the color of the lines as weights are being modified according to the last train epoch performance. Blue = positive feedback vs. black = negative feedback. The predicted value of LOS will be far off initially as the weights have been randomly initialized, but the model improves iteratively as it is exposed to more experiences. The difference between the predicted and true value is calculated as the model metric.

Back Propagation of the Error

The model optimizer updates all the weights simultaneously, according to the last metric and loss function results. The weights are slightly modified with each sample the model sees – the cost function is providing the necessary feedback from the metric that measures the distance between the recent prediction vs. the true LOS value. The optimizer basically searches for the global minimum of the loss function

This process is now repeated with the next instance (sample or batch) and so on. The model learns with each and every experience until it is trained on the whole dataset.

The cost function below shows how the model approaches the minimum with each iteration / epoch.

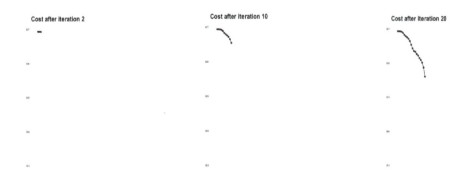

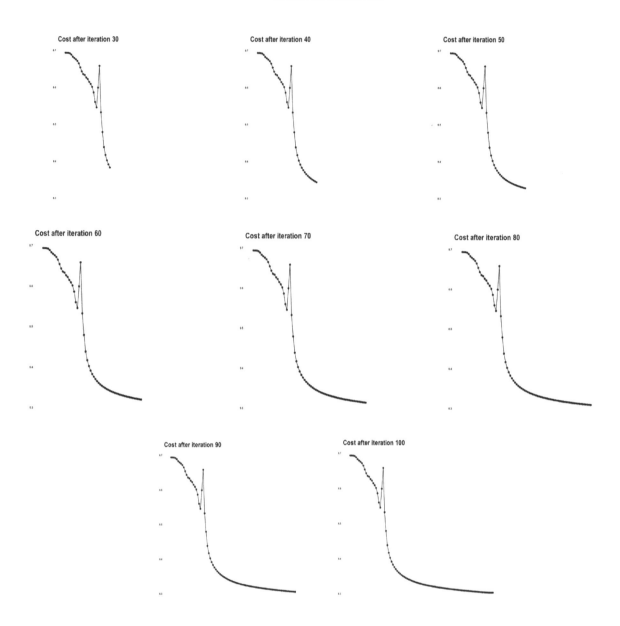

From "Coding with Data" by Tamas Szilagyi [1].

Once the training has ended, the model has a set of weights that have been exposed to 100 samples of age and BMI. These weights have been iteratively modified during the forward propagation of the input and the back propagation of errors. Now, when faced with a new, never before seen instance of age and BMI, the model can predict the LOS based on previous experiences.

Unsupervised Learning
Just because there is no output (labels) in unsupervised learning doesn't mean the model is not constrained by a loss / cost function. In the clustering algorithm from the chapter on Unsupervised Learning , for example, its cost function was the distance between each point and its cluster centroid, and the model optimizer tried to minimize this function with each iteration.

Loss / Cost Function vs. Features
We can chart the loss function (Z) vs. the input features: age (X) and BMI (Y) and follow the model as it performs a gradient descent on a nice, convex cost function that has only one (global) minimum:

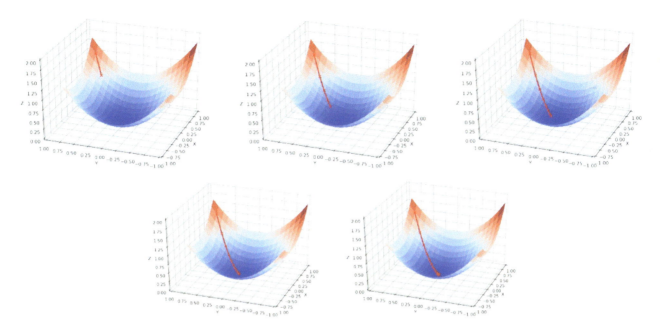

Sometimes two features can present a more complex landscape of a loss function, one with many local minima, saddles and the one, much sought after, global minimum:

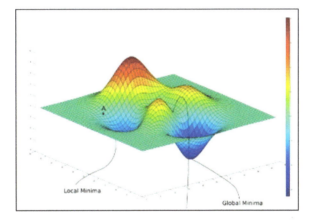

Here is a comparison of several ML model optimizers, competing to escape a saddle point on a loss function, in order to get to the optimizers' nirvana – the global minimum. Some optimizers are using a technique called momentum, which simulates a ball accumulating physical momentum as it goes down hill. Getting stuck on a saddle in hyperspace is not a good thing for a model / optimizer, as the poor red Stochastic Gradient Descent (SGD) optimizer may be able to tell, if it will ever escape:

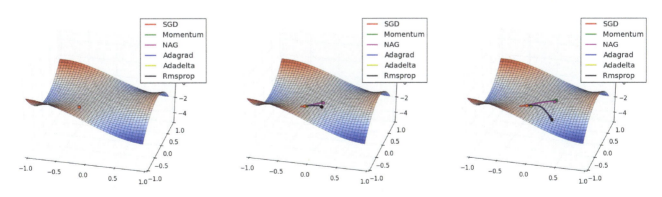

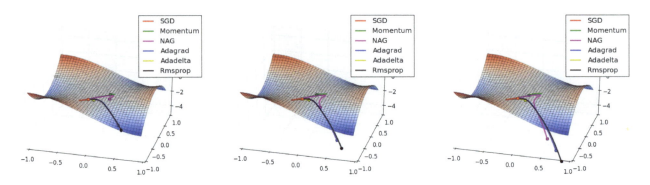

From "Behavior of adaptive learning rate algorithms at a saddle point" – NVIDIA blog [3].

Just to give you an idea of how complex a loss / cost function landscape can be, below is the loss function of VGG-56 – a known image analysis model trained on a set of several million images. This specific model loss function has as X – Y axes the two main principal components of all the features of an image. Z axis is the cost function.

The interesting landscape below is where VGG-56 has to navigate and find the global minimum – not just any minimum, but the lowest of them. Not a trivial task:

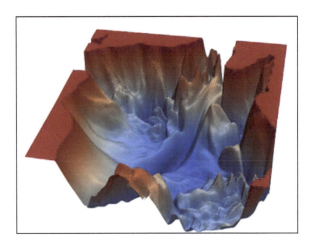

From "Intro to optimization in deep learning" – PaperSpace Blog [2].

Compressing many dimensions an image usually has, into only two (X-Y) – while minimizing the loss of variance – is usually a job performed by principal component analysis (PCA), a type of unsupervised ML algorithm. That's another aspect of ML – models that can help us visualize stuff which was unimaginable only a couple of years ago, such as the 3D map of the cost function of an image analysis algorithm.

References:
1. http://tamaszilagyi.com/blog/an-animated-neural-net-implementation/blog/
2. https://blog.paperspace.com/intro-to-optimization-in-deep-learning-gradient-descent/
3. https://devblogs.nvidia.com/introduction-neural-machine-translation-gpus-part-2/sgd_viz/

6. Artificial Neural Networks Exposed

Before detailing what is a NN, let's define what it is not.
As there is much popular debate around the question whether a NN is mimicking or simulating the human brain, I'll quote Francois Chollet, one of the luminaries in the AI field. It may help you separate at this early stage between science fiction and real science and forget any myths or preconceptions you may have had about NN:

"Nowadays the name neural network exists purely for historical reasons—it's an extremely misleading name because they're neither neural nor networks. In particular, neural networks have hardly anything to do with the brain.
A more appropriate name would have been layered representations learning or hierarchical representations learning, or maybe even deep differentiable models or chained geometric transforms, to emphasize the fact that continuous geometric space manipulation is at their core.
NN are chains of differentiable, parameterized geometric functions, trained with gradient descent."
From "Deep Learning with Python" by Francois Chollet [1].

You've met already an artificial neural network (NN) in the last chapter. It predicted the LOS based on age and BMI, using a cost function and trained with gradient descent as part of its optimizer.

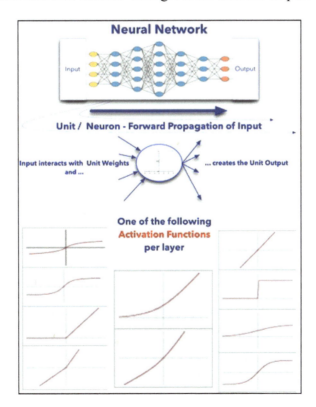

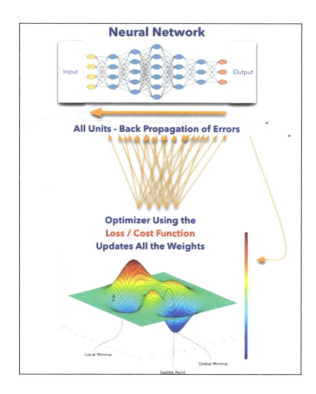

ANN Main Components

- A model has many layers: one input layer, one or more hidden layers, and one output layer.
- A layer has many units (aka neurons). Some ML models have hundreds of layers and tens of millions of units.
- Layers are interconnected in a specific architecture (dense, recurrent, convoluted, pooling, etc.)
- The output of one layer is the input of the next layer.
- Each layer has an activation function that applies to all its units (not to be confused with the loss / cost function).
- Different layers may have different activation functions.
- Each unit has its own weight.
- The overall arrangement and values of the model weights comprise the model knowledge.
- Training is done in epochs. Each epoch deals with a batch of samples from input.
- Each epoch has two steps: forward propagation of input and back propagation of errors (see above diagrams).
- A metric is calculated as the difference between the model prediction and the true value if it is a supervised learning ML model.
- An optimizer algorithm will update the weights of the model using the loss / cost function.
- The optimizer helps the model navigate the hyperspace of possibilities while minimizing the loss function and searching for its global minimum.
- After model is trained and it makes a prediction, the model uses the final values of the weights learned.

In the following example, a ML model tries to predict the type of animal in an image as a supervised classification task.

- An input layer on the left side accepts as input the image tensors as many small numbers.
- Only one hidden layer (usually there are many layers). It is fully connected to both the input and the output layers.
- An output layer on the right that predicts an animal from an image. It has the same number of output units as the number of animal types we'd like to predict. The probabilities of all the predicted animals should sum up to one or 100 percent.
-

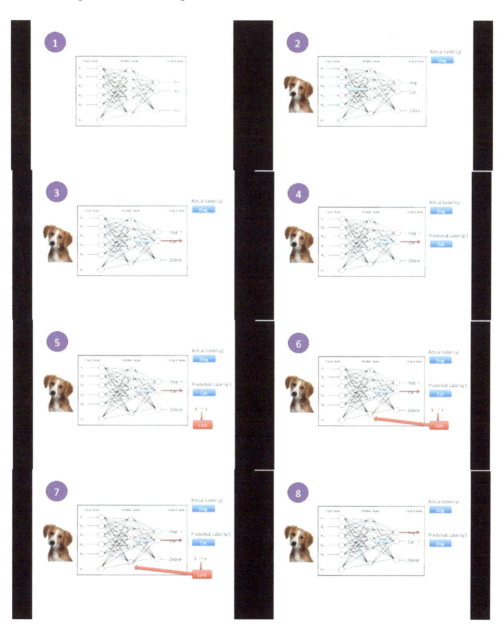

From giphy [2].

What Is the Difference Between a NN and a Non-NN ML Model?

Non NN Models:
- One set of weights for the whole model.
- Model has one function (e.g. linear regression).
- No control over model internal model architecture
- Usually do not have local minima in their loss function
- Limited hyperspace of possibilities and expressivity

NN Models:
- One to usually many layers, each layer with its own units and weights.
- Each layer has a function, not necessarily linear.
- Full control over model architecture.
- May have multiple minima as the loss function is more complex.
- Can represent a more complex hypothesis hyperspace.

Remember the clustering exercise from a previous chapter?

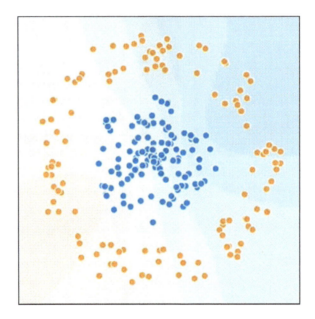

Task: given the X and Y coordinate of a dot, predict the dot color.
Experience: X and Y coordinates.
Output: color of dot.
Performance: accuracy of prediction.

How would a NN model approach the above supervised learning problem ?

Note that no centroids are defined, nor the number of classes (two in the above case) are given.
The loss function that the model tries to optimize results from the accuracy metric defined: predicted vs. real values (blue or orange). Below there are five units (neurons) in the hidden layer and two units in the output layer (actually one unit to decide if yes / no blue for example, would suffice as the decision is binary, either blue or orange.)

The model is exposed to the input in batches. Each unit makes its own calculation and the result is a probability of blue or orange. After summarizing all the layers, the model predicts a dot color. If wrong, the weights are modified in one direction. If right, in the opposite direction (notice the neurons modifying their weights during training). Eventually, the model learns to predict the dot color by a given pair of X and Y (X1 and X2 in the figures below)

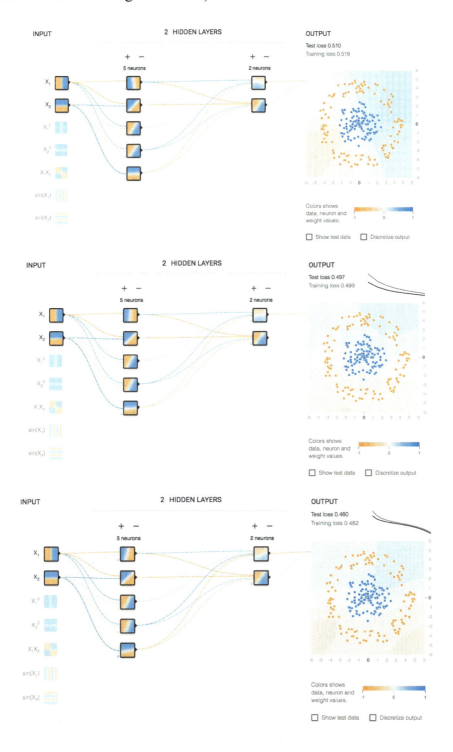

Alexander Scarlat MD

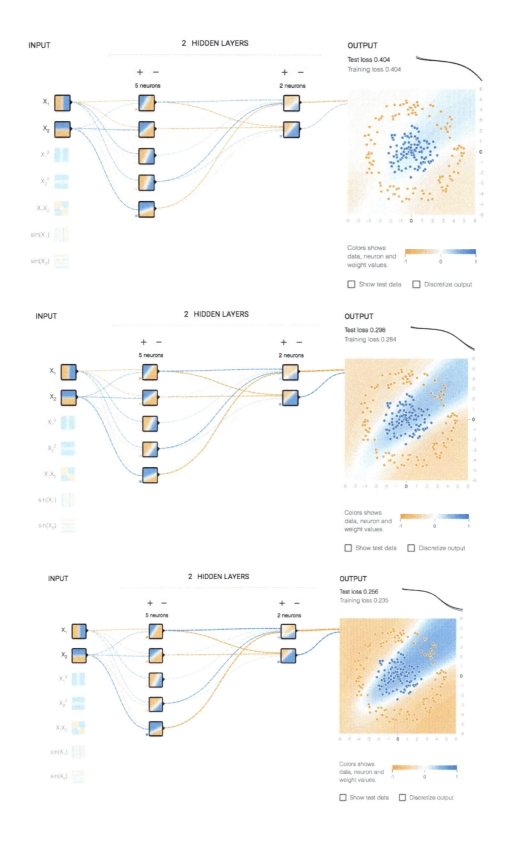

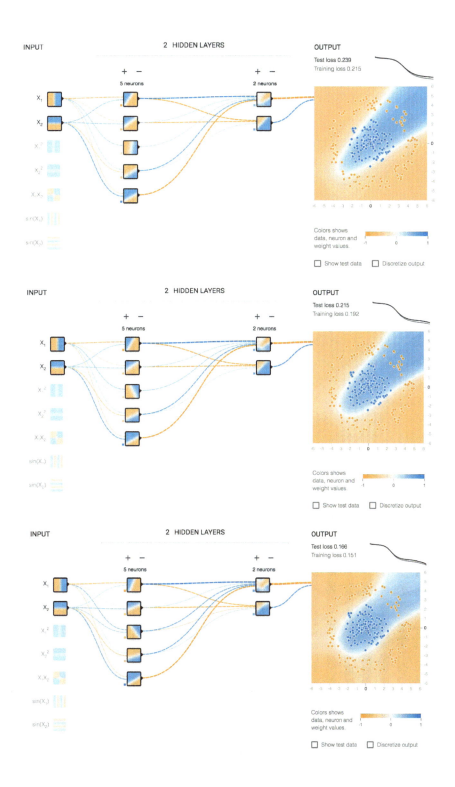

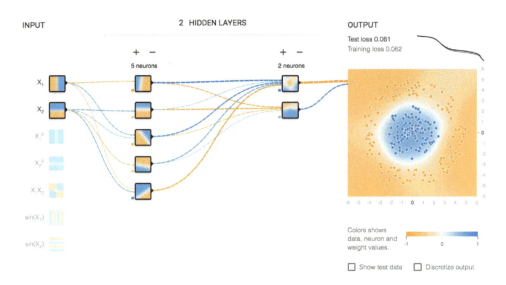

From "My First Weekend of Deep Learning at Floyd Hub" [3].

Advantages of a NN Over a Non-NN ML Model

- Having activation functions, most of them non-linear, increases the model capability to deal with more complex, non-linear problems.
- Chaining units in a NN is analogous to chaining functions and the result is a definitely more complex, composite model function.
- NN can represent more complex hypothesis hyperspace than non-NN model. NN is more expressive.
- NN offers full control over the architecture: number of layers, number of units in a layer, their activation functions, etc.
- The densely connected model introduced above is only one of the many NN architectures used.
- Deep learning, for example, uses other NN architectures: convoluted, recurrent, pooling, etc. (to be explained later in this book). Model may have a combination of several basic architectures (e.g. dense on top of a convoluted and pooling).
- Transfer learning. A trained NN model can be transferred with all its weights, architecture, etc. and used for other than the original intended purpose of the model.

The last point of transfer learning, which I'll detail in future chapters, is one of the most exciting developments in the field of AI. It allows a model to apply previously learned knowledge and skills (a.k.a. model weights and architecture) with only minor modifications to new situations. A model trained to identify animals, slightly modified, can be used to identify flowers.

References:
1. https://www.amazon.com/Deep-Learning-Python-Francois-Chollet/dp/1617294438
2. https://giphy.com/gifs/neural-networks-sq7yhyvOg031S
3. https://blog.floydhub.com/my-first-weekend-of-deep-learning/

7. Controlling the Machine Learning Process

We'd like a ML model to learn from past experiences, so post-training, it should be able to generalize when predicting an output based on unseen data. The ML model capacity should not be too small nor too large for the task at hand, as both situations are not helping to achieve the goal of generalization.

Under and Overfitting

In the funny yet accurate description below:

- Knowledge sits in some form, but a ML model with not enough capacity will fail to see any relationships in the data.
- Experience is the capability to connect the proverbial dots. Once a ML model achieves this level, training should stop. Otherwise,
- Overfitting is when the model tries to impress us with its creativity. The ML model just had too much training and is now overdoing it:

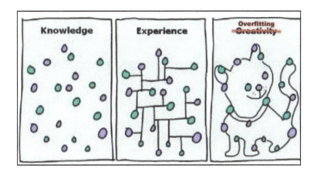

From Algotrading 101 [1].

Regression and Classification Examples of Under / Overfitting

We are searching for the sweet spot — a good, robust fit so the model would be able to generalize with unseen data. The model should have sufficient capacity to be able to learn and improve and yet at the same time, not necessarily become the absolute best AI student on the training set.

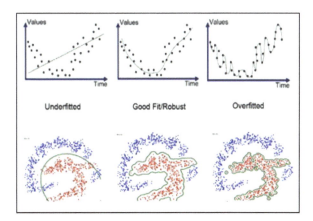

Modified from "Towards Data Sciences" [2].

Underfitting
Consider the left side of the above figure:

- The upper diagram displays data which is obviously not linear. Still, the ML model we've applied is linearly restricted – the model capacity is limited for the task.
- The lower diagram displays a classification task, but the model is restricted to a circle. Its capacity is limited, so it cannot classify the dots better than with a circle separation line

When a ML model is underfitting, it basically doesn't have enough or the right type of brain power for the task at hand or the model is exposed to a poor choice of features during training. We can help the ML model by:

- Using non-linear, more complex models.
- Increase the number of layers and / or units in a NN.
- Adding more features.
- Engineering more complex features from existing ones (using BMI instead of weight and height).

Underfitting is also called high bias and low variance and is one of the causes for a model to underperform. The model has a high bias towards a linear solution (in the regression example above) and a low variance in terms of limited variability of the features learned

Overfitting
You've trained your ML model for some time now and it achieves an amazing performance on the training set. Unfortunately, once in production, the ML model is only slightly better than just random predictions. What happened?

As the right side of the above figure shows, the model has used its large capacity to memorize the whole training set. The ML model became a memory bank for the training samples' features, similar to a database. This overfitting caused the model to over train, to become "creative," and also to become the best-ever on the training data.

However, the overfitted model fails on real-life test data because it has lost the ability to generalize. We need the ML model to learn with each experience to generalize, not to become a memory bank

Overfitting is also called low bias and high variance, as the model has a low bias to any specific solution (linear, polynomial, etc.). The model will consider anything, any function, and it has a huge variance. Both factors contribute to an increased overall model prediction error:

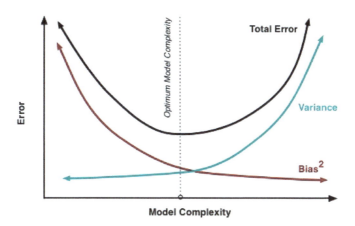

From Dataquest.io [3]

How do we achieve a balance between the above two opposing forces of bias and variance? We need a tool to monitor the learning process — the learning curves — and a method to continuously test our model at each and every epoch, the cross-validation technique.

Training, Validation, and Testing Sets

Once you've got the data for a ML project, it is customary to cut a random 20 percent of samples, the test set and put it aside, never to be looked at again until the time of testing. Any transformation you plan on doing (imputing missing values, cleaning, normalizing, etc.) should be done separately on the training and test sets.

This strict separation will easily prevent the scenario where normalizing over the whole data set and learning the average and standard deviation of the test set in the process may influence the model decision making in a way similar to cheating or letting the model know information about the test set, which the model should not know. The rest of the data after removal of this test set is the original training set.

As the model is going to be exposed to the training data multiple times — with different hyper-parameters (see below), architectures, etc. — if we allow the model to "see" the test data repeatedly, the model will eventually learn the test set as well. We want to prevent the model from memorizing all the data and especially to prevent the model exposure to the test set .

The original training set is used in a cross-validation scheme, so the same training set can be used also for validating each learning epoch. In a fivefold cross-validation scheme, we create each epoch, a 80 percent subset from the original training set and a validation set from the remaining 20 percent. Basically, we create a mini-test set for each learning epoch — a validation set — and we move this validation set within the original train set with each learning epoch (experiment in the figure below):

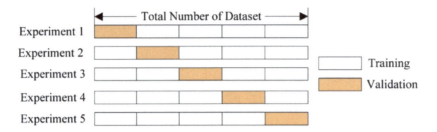

From Kaggle [4].

Learning Curves

With a cross-validation arrangement as detailed above, we can monitor the learning process and identify any pathological behavior on behalf of our student ML model during training:

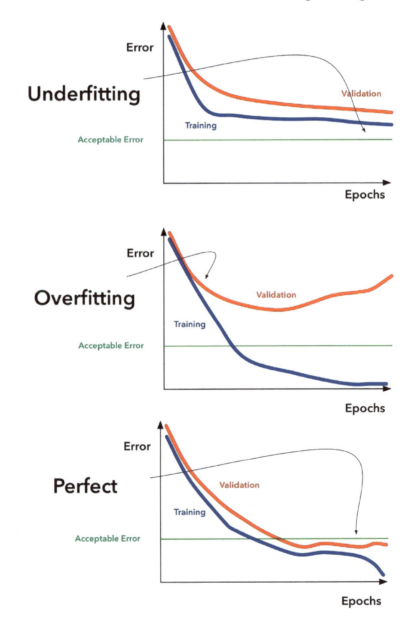

Underfitting learning curves above show both the training and the validation curves remaining above the acceptable error threshold during the epochs of the learning process. Basically the model does not learn: either there's not enough model capacity or not good, representative enough features it can generalize upon. We need to either increase model capacity, increase the number or complexity of the features, or both. Adding more training samples will not help.

Overfitting learning curves show that pretty early during the learning process, the model started overfitting, when the two learning curves separate. The training curve continued to improve and reduce the training error, while the validation curve stopped showing improvement and actually started to deteriorate. Decreasing the model capacity, decreasing the number of features, or increasing the number of samples may help.

Perfect fit happens when the validation error is below the acceptable threshold and it starts to plateau and separate from the training curve. At that number of training epochs, we should stop, call an end for the learning session, and give our ML model a short class break.

Learning Rate

A ML model has parameters (weights) and hyper-parameters such as the learning rate.

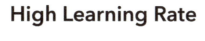

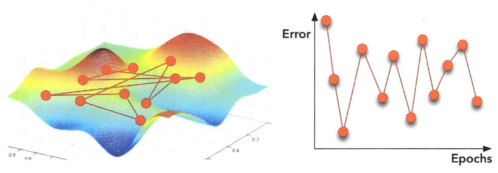

With a too-low learning rate, the model will take its time to find the global minimum of the cost function (top part in the above figure).

Too high a learning rate will cause the model will miss the global minimum because it jumps around in too large steps. Modern optimizers can automatically modify their learning rate as they approach the minimum in order not to miss it with a too large jump above it.

Data Augmentation

Usually collecting more samples to feed an overfitting model is a time, money, and resource-consuming activity. Consider an image analysis ML model that identifies between dogs and cats in an image. Until recently, this exercise was used by CAPTCHA to distinguish between humans and malicious bots trying to impersonate humans. Machines recently achieved the same level as humans, so CAPTCHA is not using this challenge any more. Nevertheless, dogs vs. cats became one of the basic, introductory exercises in computer vision / image analysis.

While developing such an image classification model, one usually increases the model capacity gradually until the model starts overfitting. Then its customary to add data augmentation, a technique used only on the training set, in which images are being reformatted randomly around the following image parameters:

- Zoom
- Scale
- Brightness
- Skew
- Mirror around vertical / horizontal axes
- Colors

By exposing the algorithm during training to a more diverse range of images, the ML model will start overfitting at a much later epoch, as the training set is more complex than the validation set. This in turn will allow the model to bring the validation error to an acceptable level.

Data augmentation allows a ML model to realize that a cat looking to the right side is still a cat if it looks to the left side. With data augmentation, the ML model will learn to generalize that a dog is still a dog if it is scaled to 80 percent, flipped horizontally, and skewed by 20 degrees. No animals were harmed during this data augmentation exercise:

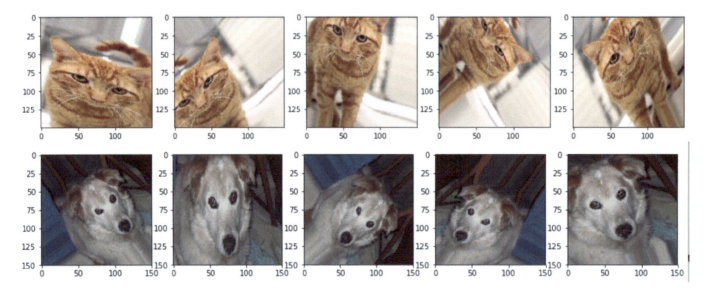

Regularizers

Eventually, a big enough model will start overfitting the data, even if the training set has been augmented. Another technique to deal with overfitting is to use a regularizer, a model hyper-parameter. Basically it penalizes the model loss function on any large modifications to the model weights. Keeping the changes to the weights within small limits during each epoch is important, as we don't want the model to literally "jump to any conclusions."

Dropout

An interesting, different, and surprisingly very efficient approach to overfitting that can prevent a ML model from learning the whole training set by heart is called dropout. Like data augmentation above, dropout technique is used only on the training set. It takes out randomly up to 50 percent of a NN layer units from one learning epoch, like randomly sending home half of the students for one class. How can this strategy prevent overfitting?

The analogy with these students being dismissed from that class / epoch caused all the other units (students) in the layer to work harder and learn features they were not supposed to learn otherwise. This in turn zeroed the weights for up to half of the units while forcing other units to modify their weights in a way that is not conducive towards a "memory bank." Shortly, dropout destroys any nascent memory bank a ML model may try to create during training.

Testing

Once training is completed, hyper-parameters have been optimized, data has been re-engineered, the model has been iteratively corrected, etc. then and only then, one brings out the hidden testing set. We test the ML model and its performance on the test set will hopefully be close to its real-life performance.

References:

1. https://algotrading101.com/blog/1543426/what-is-curve-fitting-overfitting-in-trading-optimization
2. https://towardsdatascience.com/overfitting-vs-underfitting-a-conceptual-explanation-d94ee20ca7f9
3. https://www.dataquest.io/blog/learning-curves-machine-learning/
4. https://www.kaggle.com/dansbecker/cross-validation

8. Predict Hospital Mortality

In this chapter we'll walk thru our first, end-to-end ML workflow, while predicting the hospital mortality of ICU patients. The Python code I've used for this chapter, is publicly available at Kaggle [1].
The data for this exercise is a subset of MIMIC3 - *Multiparameter Intelligent Monitoring in Intensive Care* - a de-identified, ICU, freely available database from Physionet [2].
MIMIC3 is a RDBMS (Relational Database Management System) with many tables and relationships and information on approximately 59k admissions. As no ML model will digest data in a relational format, the first step is to decide how to flatten the relational structure, so each instance will represent one admission.

Hypothesis on the Number of Patient-Hospital Interactions
One can learn a lot about the patient's outcome from the number of interactions a patient has with the hospital: number of labs, orders, meds, imaging reports, etc. Not necessarily the quality of these interactions (abnormal or normal, degree of abnormality, etc.) - just their numbers. It is of course, an oversimplification of the patient outcome prediction problem, but it is an easier toy-model to explain compared to a full-blown production-ready model.
We'll present the ML model with the daily average of interactions, such as the daily average number of labs, meds, consultations, etc. In real life with this arrangement, the ML model can predict mortality each and every day as the average number of interactions between patient and hospital changes daily.

Flatten MIMIC Into a Table
Using a method detailed in my second book *Medical Information Extraction & Analysis: From Zero to Hero with a Bit of SQL and a Real-life Database* [3], I've summarized MIMIC3 into one table with 58,976 instances - each row representing one admission. This table has the following columns:

- Age, Gender, Admission Type, Admission Source

Daily average number of:

- Diagnosis
- Procedures
- Labs
- Microbiology labs
- Input and output events (eg: any modification to an IV drip)
- Prescriptions and Orders
- Chart events
- Procedural Events (eg: insertion of an arterial line)
- Callouts for consultation
- Notes (including nursing, MD notes, radiology reports)
- Transfers between care units
- Total number of daily interactions between the patient and the hospital - summary of all the above

The hospital mortality is the label of the set - the outcome we'd like the ML model to predict in this supervised learning, binary classification exercise.

Prepare the Data

As previously detailed, I've imputed the missing values with either the average, the most frequent value or just "na":

	gender	age	LOSdays	admit_type	admit_location	AdmitDiagnosis	insurance	religion	marital_status	ethnicity	NumCallouts	NumDiagnosis	NumProcs	AdmitProcedui
0	F	35	6.17	EMERGENCY	CLINIC REFERRAL/PREMATURE	DIABETIC KETOACIDOSIS	Private	PROTESTANT QUAKER	DIVORCED	WHITE	0.16	2.59	0.00	na
1	M	59	4.04	EMERGENCY	EMERGENCY ROOM ADMIT	UPPER GI BLEED	Private	NOT SPECIFIED	SINGLE	WHITE	0.25	2.23	0.99	Endosc control hem
2	F	48	12.04	EMERGENCY	EMERGENCY ROOM ADMIT	COPD FLARE	Private	NOT SPECIFIED	SINGLE	BLACK/AFRICAN AMERICAN	0.00	0.75	0.17	Non-invasive n vent
3	F	73	7.29	EMERGENCY	EMERGENCY ROOM ADMIT	BOWEL OBSTRUCTION	Private	JEWISH	MARRIED	WHITE	0.41	0.69	0.27	Part sm bowel resect NEC
4	M	60	4.88	EMERGENCY	TRANSFER FROM HOSP/EXTRAM	CORONARY ARTERY DISEASE	Private	CATHOLIC	MARRIED	WHITE	0.00	3.69	0.82	Aortocor bypas cor art
5	F	54	4.38	ELECTIVE	PHYS REFERRAL/NORMAL DELI	RENAL MASS LEFT/SDA	Private	EPISCOPALIAN	MARRIED	WHITE	0.23	1.14	0.68	Nephrouretere
6	M	21	14.38	EMERGENCY	CLINIC REFERRAL/PREMATURE	MOTOR VEHICLE ACCIDENT WITH UNSPECIFIED INJURIES	Medicaid	NOT SPECIFIED	SINGLE	HISPANIC OR LATINO	0.07	0.97	1.04	Debrid opn fx-l
7	M	67	10.08	EMERGENCY	TRANSFER FROM HOSP/EXTRAM	CORONARY ARTERY DISEASE	Medicare	CATHOLIC	MARRIED	WHITE	0.10	1.09	0.40	1 int mam-cor bypass
8	F	49	0.63	ELECTIVE	PHYS REFERRAL/NORMAL DELI	RIGHT SHOULDER ADHESIVE CAPSULITIS/SDA	Medicaid	CATHOLIC	SINGLE	WHITE	0.00	12.70	4.76	Rep recur shldi disloc
9	M	55	6.17	EMERGENCY	CLINIC REFERRAL/PREMATURE	PNEUMONIA	Medicare	PROTESTANT QUAKER	SINGLE	WHITE	0.00	1.78	0.81	Temporary tracheostomy

Summary of some basic stats:

	age	LOSdays	NumCallouts	NumDiagnosis	NumProcs	NumCPTevents	NumInput	NumLabs	NumMicroLabs	NumNotes	NumOutput	NumRx	NumProcEvents	NumTransfers	NumChartE
count	58976.000000	58976.000000	58976.000000	58976.00000	58976.000000	58976.000000	58976.000000	58976.000000	58976.000000	58976.000000	58976.000000	58976.000000	58976.000000	58976.000000	58976.0000
mean	53.005884	10.114955	0.099374	2.67596	0.785599	1.074118	30.379017	46.421124	1.219913	6.464789	7.111594	9.593702	0.691903	1.093313	528.50517
std	26.028120	12.456231	0.163437	8.26559	3.558090	2.027148	62.430163	76.061561	4.236693	106.709903	7.551822	12.601338	2.117615	3.169441	640.25006
min	0.000000	0.000000	0.000000	0.00000	0.000000	0.000000	0.000000	0.000000	0.000000	0.000000	0.000000	0.000000	0.000000	0.000000	0.000000
25%	43.000000	3.710000	0.000000	0.82000	0.210000	0.000000	4.850000	26.980000	0.160000	0.140000	1.750000	4.330000	0.000000	0.380000	207.41000
50%	59.000000	6.460000	0.000000	1.41000	0.420000	0.970000	13.990000	38.520000	0.510000	0.330000	5.310000	8.370000	0.000000	0.650000	417.87500
75%	73.000000	11.790000	0.160000	2.40000	0.710000	1.560000	34.360000	50.860000	1.350000	0.770000	10.490000	12.270000	0.880000	1.060000	700.30250
max	89.000000	294.630000	4.760000	450.00000	275.000000	225.000000	6825.000000	5175.000000	375.000000	7500.000000	375.000000	750.000000	100.000000	125.000000	49325.000(

Leaking Data from the Future

LOS was eliminated from the dataset as it is never a good idea to provide the model information from the future. When asked to predict mortality, the LOS is not yet known - so it should not be given to the model during training.

Leaking data to the ML model is equivalent to cheating yourself - the model will have a stellar performance in the lab and a terrible one in real life.

Skewed Data and Normalization

Histogram of age and the number of patients in each category:

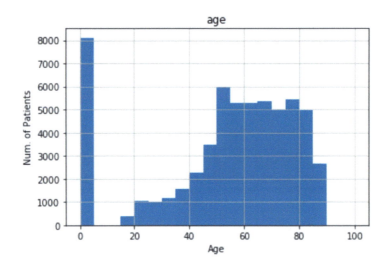

The raw data in the above chart is skewed (eg. there are newborns but no other pediatric patients in MIMIC3, there's also a sharp cut-off at the age of 90). This is partially corrected during the normalization process, the same parameter - age - after normalization:

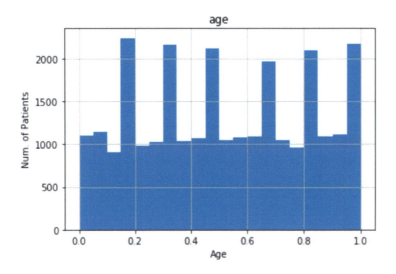

The process of normalization was applied to all the features.

Mortality and Imbalanced Datasets

The in-hospital mortality of the patients in MIMIC3 dataset is 5,855 / 58,967 = 9.93% of admissions.

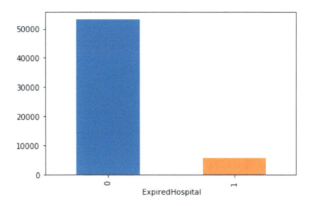

This is considered an imbalanced dataset as the classes of Lived vs Expired are imbalanced 9:1. Consider a simple, dumb "model": one that always predicts the patient lives and it assumes 0% mortality.
Accuracy is defined as (True Positives + True Negatives) / All samples, so this "model" has a fantastic accuracy of 90% on MIMIC3 dataset: With 100 patients and a model predicting that all patients lived, TN=90 and FN=10, the accuracy is (0+90)/100=90%. If you need more confusion about TP, FP, TN, FN and their derivatives, please do explore the fascinating confusion matrix [4].

This exercise with a dumb "model" provides the necessary perspective on the problem, as it gives us a certain baseline to compare against the machine. We know by now that a 90% accuracy is not such a high goal to achieve. It's considered common sense in ML to try come up with a sanity check, a baseline against which to compare a metric - *before* - we measure the machine performance on a task.

When a problem involves a moderate to highly imbalanced classes situation - such as mortality in our dataset being 10% - accuracy is not the only metric to monitor, as it may be quite misleading. The relevance of the predictions is an important parameter as well:

Precision = TP/(TP+FN)
How many selected items were relevant ?
With our dumb "model" precision is 0, as no True Positives (TP) have been selected (0/0+10)

Recall = TP/TP+FP
How many relevant items are selected ?
Recall for this "model" is also 0, as nothing predicted was relevant (actually recall is indeterminate 0/0)

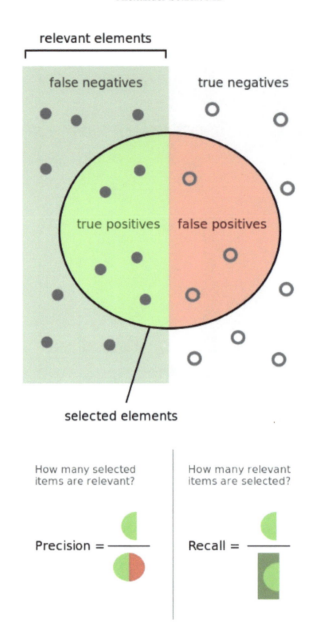

From Wikipedia [5]

One Metric Only

A ML model needs one, and only one metric to use for calculations of the loss function and optimizer. The model will refuse to work if presented with two metrics, such as precision and recall. In the case of imbalanced classes, precision and recall have one prodigy, named F1 score - the harmonic mean of precision and recall. A higher F1 score is better.

In the following examples I've used accuracy, precision, recall and F1 score as the models' metrics for optimization - but only one metric at a time.
In addition, I've also optimized the models on the Area Under the Curve (AUC) of the Receiver Operating Characteristic (ROC), even though ROC AUC is best used with balanced classes. A higher AUC is better. From Wikipedia [6].

Task: predict mortality as a supervised learning classification based on a binary decision - yes / no
Experience: MIMIC3 subset detailed above
Performance: Accuracy, F1 score and ROC AUC

The original dataset was split into two subsets as previously explained:

- Training: 47,180 instances or samples, admissions
- Testing:11,796 instances

Models

Initially I've trained and cross-evaluated 7 classifier models: Logistic Regression, Random Forest, Stochastic Gradient Descent, K-Nearest Neighbors, Decision Tree, Gaussian Naive Bayes, Support Vector Machine. These models have used the various metrics detailed above for their optimization algorithms - one metric at a time.

The best model came as Random Forest Classifier with the following learning curves while optimizing on ROC AUC:

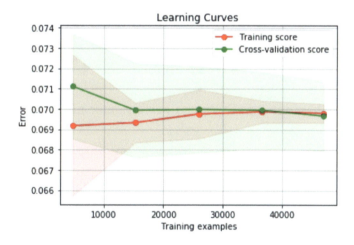

The confusion matrix for the Random Forest Classifier (RF) model on the test subset of 11,796 samples, never seen before by the RF model:

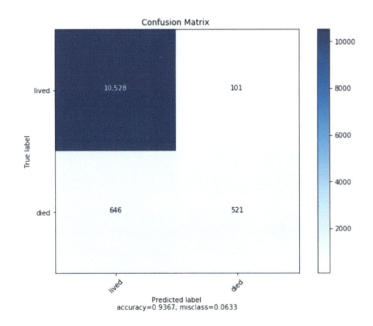

- TN: 10528
- FP: 101
- FN: 646
- TP: 521

The above confusion matrix translates into the following performance metrics for the RF model:

- Accuracy 93.7%
- Precision 83.9%
- Recall 44.4%
- F1 score 0.581
- AUC 0.717

Feature Importance

We can ask the RF model to display the most important features in the data, that helped the algorithm in the decision making process about hospital mortality:

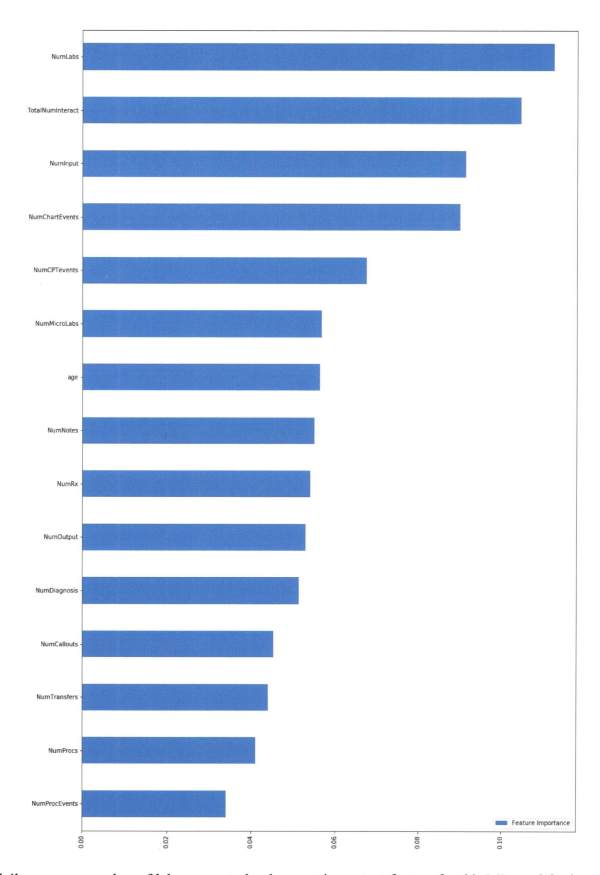

The daily average number of labs seems to be the most important feature for this ML model, almost twice more important than the age parameter.

Note that 6 features are more important in predicting the admission mortality than the patient's age:

	Feature Importance
NumLabs	0.112276
TotalNumInteract	0.104491
NumInput	0.091187
NumChartEvents	0.089801
NumCPTevents	0.067360
NumMicroLabs	0.056735
age	0.056312
NumNotes	0.055065
NumRx	0.054031
NumOutput	0.052889
NumDiagnosis	0.051408
NumCallouts	0.045222
NumTransfers	0.044012
NumProcs	0.041014
NumProcEvents	0.034039
EMERGENCY	0.006705
EMERGENCY ROOM ADMIT	0.006496
M	0.005879
F	0.005050
TRANSFER FROM HOSP/EXTRAM	0.004447
CLINIC REFERRAL/PREMATURE	0.004072
PHYS REFERRAL/NORMAL DELI	0.003602

I've tested several Neural Network architectures and the best results came from a NN with 3 layers fully inter connected (dense) of 2048 units each.

The output sigmoid unit produces a probability between 0 and 1. If this last unit output is above 0.5, the ML model will predict that the patient died. If the output is below 0.5, the model will predict that the patient lived.

Overall the NN had 8.4M trainable parameters. In order to prevent overfitting, I've employed dropout and regularizers with a relatively slow learning rate, as explained in the last chapter. The NN training and validation learning curves showing model overfitting after approximately 55 epochs:

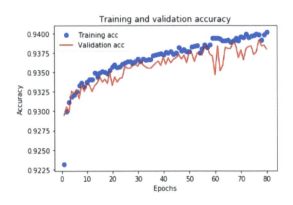

The confusion matrix for the above NN model on the test subset of 11,796 samples, never seen before by the model:

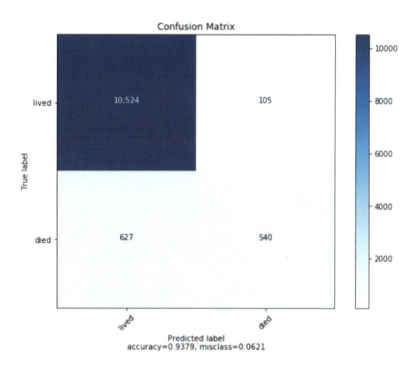

- TN: 10524
- FP: 105
- FN: 627
- TP: 540

The above confusion matrix translates into the following performance metrics for the RF model:

- Accuracy 93.8%
- Precision 83.7%
- Recall 46.3%
- F1 score 0.596
- AUC 0.726

A comparison between RF and NN performances on the prediction of hospital mortality:

	Random Forest	NN
Accuracy	93.7%	93.8%
Precision	83.9%	83.7%
Recall	44.4%	46.3%
F1 score	0.581	0.596
ROC AUC	0.717	0.726

Next time you are impressed by a high accuracy of a prediction made by a ML model, remember that high accuracy may be accompanied by very low precision and recall, especially with problems where the data classes are imbalanced. In such cases, politely ask for the additional metrics: confusion matrix, Precision, Recall, F1 score and AUC.

As a sanity check, always try to estimate what a No-ML-No-AI kind of "model" would have predicted in the same situation. Use this estimate as the first baseline to test your ML model against.

References:

1. https://www.kaggle.com/drscarlat/predict-hospital-mortality-mimic3
2. https://mimic.physionet.org/
3. https://www.amazon.com/dp/1544093373/ref=sr_1_2?s=books&ie=UTF8&qid=1521489772&sr=1-2
4. https://en.wikipedia.org/wiki/Confusion_matrix
5. https://en.wikipedia.org/wiki/Precision_and_recall
6. https://en.wikipedia.org/wiki/Receiver_operating_characteristic

9. Predict Length of Stay (LOS)

In this chapter we'll walk thru another, end-to-end ML workflow, while predicting the hospital LOS of ICU patients.

The data is a subset of MIMIC3 - Multiparameter Intelligent Monitoring in Intensive Care - a de-identified, ICU, freely available database from Physionet [1]. Using a recipe detailed in my second book Medical Information Extraction & Analysis: From Zero to Hero with a Bit of SQL and a Real-life Database [2], I've summarized MIMIC3 into one table with 58,976 instances - each row representing one admission. This table has the following columns, similar to the last chapter:

- Age, Gender, Admission Type, Admission Source

Daily average number of:

- Diagnosis
- Procedures
- Labs
- Microbiology labs
- Input and output events (eg: any modification to an IV drip)
- Prescriptions and Orders
- Chart events
- Procedural Events (eg: insertion of an arterial line)
- Callouts for consultation
- Notes (including nursing, MD notes, radiology reports)
- Transfers between care units
- Total number of daily interactions between the patient and the hospital - summary of all the above

Using the daily averages of interactions allows the ML model to predict the LOS on a daily basis - as these averages are being modified on a daily basis.

I've removed mortality from this dataset as I don't want to provide any hints to the model in the form of mortality = short LOS. Besides, when asked to predict LOS the model should not be aware of the overall admission outcome in terms of mortality, as it may be considered data leaked from the future.

The Hospital LOS in days is the label of the dataset - the outcome we'd like the ML model to predict in this supervised learning exercise. We will approach the LOS prediction challenge in two ways:
- **Regression** to arbitrary values - predict the actual number of days a specific admission is associated with
- **Classification** to several groups - predict to which class the admission belongs to (eg. low, medium, high, very high LOS)

Short LOS Is Not Always a Good Outcome

Please keep in mind that a short LOS is not necessarily a good outcome - as the patient may have died and thus a short LOS. In addition there may be circumstances where a shorter LOS is accompanied by a higher readmission rate. In order to get the full picture, one needs to know the mortality and readmission rates associated with a specific LOS.

LOS - Regression

Task: predict the number of days in hospital for an admission
Experience: MIMIC3 subset detailed above
Performance: Mean Absolute Error (MAE) between prediction and true LOS

The Python code used for predicting LOS with regression ML models, is publicly available at Kaggle [3].

Data was separated into a train (47,180 admissions) and test (11.796 admissions) datasets as previously explained.

I've trained and cross-evaluated 12 regressor models: Gradient Boosting Regressor, Extra Trees Regressor, Random Forest Regressor, Bayesian Ridge, Ridge, Kernel Ridge, Linear SVR, SVR, Elastic Net, Lasso, SGD Regressor, Linear Regression.
The best model - Random Forest Regressor (RFR) - came on top with a Mean Absolute Error (MAE) of 1.45 days (normalized MAE of 11.8%). This performance was measured on the test subset, data the model has never seen during training.

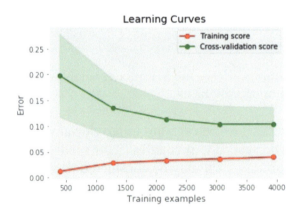

The learning curves show that the model is overfitting, as the validation MAE is stuck on approximately 0.12 or 12% while the error on the training set is much lower at 5%. Thus, the model would benefit from more samples, better features' engineering or both.

Features Importance

RFR offers a view into its decision making process by showing the most important features related to LOS:

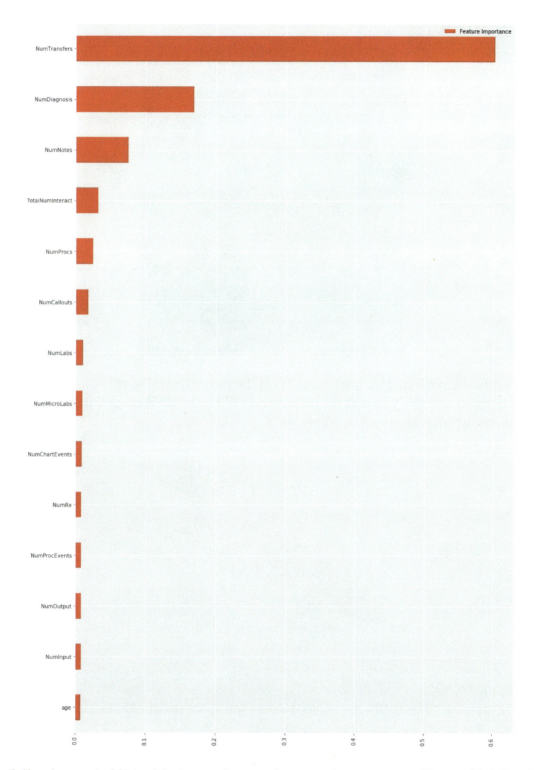

Note in the following sorted list of features, that age is not an important predictor of LOS, relative to the other features.

For example, the number of daily notes is about 10 times more important as a predictor than age, while the daily average number of transfers - the best LOS predictor - is approximately 85 times more important than age:

	Feature Importance
NumTransfers	0.601096
NumDiagnosis	0.168837
NumNotes	0.074716
TotalNumInteract	0.032215
NumProcs	0.024379
NumCallouts	0.017789
NumLabs	0.010450
NumMicroLabs	0.009337
NumChartEvents	0.008350
NumRx	0.008291
NumProcEvents	0.008283
NumOutput	0.007621
NumInput	0.007590
age	0.007464
NumCPTevents	0.006431
EMERGENCY ROOM ADMIT	0.001267

Below is the chart of the predicted vs. the true LOS on the test dataset. On the X axis are the number of real days in the hospital and the Y axis is the predicted LOS by the RFR model. In a perfect situation all points would fall on the blue identity line where X=Y:

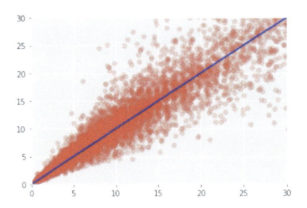

Neural Network (NN)

I've trained and evaluated several NN on the above data set: from small 15k to 20M weights in different combinations of dense layers and units (a.k.a. neurons).
One of the NN (with 12.6M trainable parameters) learning curves:

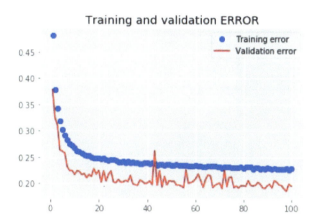

The best NN MAE is 2.39 days or a normalized MAE of 19.5%. The NN performance is worse when compared to the RFR model.

LOS - Classification

The Python code used for this part of the chapter, is publicly available at Kaggle [4].
Using the same dataset as the one used for regression above, I've grouped the admissions into the following four classes:

1. Between 0 and 4 days LOS (group 0 in the chart below)
2. Between 4 and 8
3. Between 8 and 12
4. More than 12 days of LOS (group 3 below)

Task: predict the LOS group from the four classes defined above (0,1,2,3)
Experience: same MIMIC3 subset used above, with the daily averages of interactions between patient and hospital
Performance: Accuracy, F1 score, ROC AUC as explained in the previous chapter

I've evaluated the following classifiers: Logistic Regression, Random Forest, Stochastic Gradient, K-Nearest Neighbors, Decision Tree, Support Vector Machine.
The best classifier model came (again) the Random Forest Classifier (RFC) - an ensemble of weak predictors. Below is the RFC confusion matrix on the test dataset:

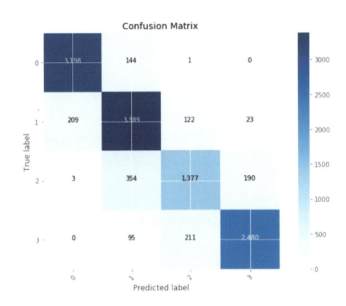

The above confusion matrix shows the predicted vs. true labels for all the 4 LOS groups.
We cannot use such a confusion matrix for calculating precision, recall, F1 and AUC as these metrics require a simpler, 2 X 2 confusion matrix with TP, FP, TN and FN. We need to calculate for each one of the four LOS groups - its own confusion matrix and derived metrics.

Each one of these classes is going to be compared against all the other groups - thus the name of the technique: *one-vs.-all* - so the results can be summarized in a 2 X 2 confusion matrix:

- TP = model predicted a class X and it was truly class X
- TN = model predicted it's not class X and it was not X
- FP = model predicted it's class X but it was not X
- FN = model predicted it is not class X, and it actually was X

In the following figure, we consider only one class, the second one, labeled 1 (as counting starts with 0) and calculate the confusion matrix of the model in regard to this class:

One-vs-All
Consider one class vs all the others

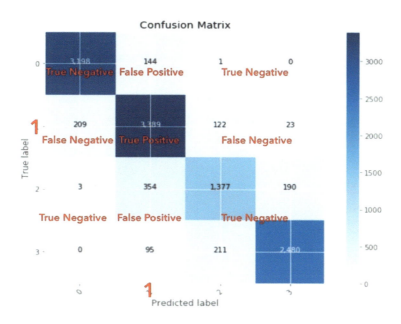

After we repeat the above exercise four times (as the number of classes) - we end up with four confusion matrices, one for each class.

We can now summarize these four confusion matrices and calculate the overall performance of the RFC model as well as compare the performance related to each one of the LOS groups:

Random Forest Classifier

	LOS group 0	LOS group 1	LOS group 2	LOS group 3	Overall
Accuracy	0.9716	0.923	0.9246	0.9552	0.9436
Recall	0.9608	0.9081	0.7053	0.8966	0.8677
Precision	0.9403	0.8577	0.8082	0.9123	0.8796
F1 score	0.9504	0.8822	0.7533	0.9044	0.8726
AUC					0.9147

The higher the F1 score and AUC - the better is the model performance.
The best NN model (with approx. 12.6M trainable parameters) performance in comparison:

NN

	LOS group 0	LOS group 1	LOS group 2	LOS group 3	Overall
Accuracy	0.9488	0.8927	0.9053	0.9406	0.9219
Recall	0.9249	0.8552	0.6715	0.8496	0.8253
Precision	0.8975	0.8155	0.7271	0.8935	0.8334
F1 score	0.911	0.8349	0.6982	0.871	0.8288
AUC					0.8861

Both the RFC and the NN models are performing best when evaluated on the first group-vs-all: LOS below vs. above 4 days (LOS group 0).

Random Forest - is an ensemble of other weak predictor models. Still it out-performs any NN by a large margin with both the regression and classification challenges of predicting the LOS. It is interesting how a group of under performing "students" manage to use their error diversity in achieving a better outcome than the best-in-class NN models.

References:

1. https://mimic.physionet.org/
2. https://www.amazon.com/dp/1544093373/ref=sr_1_2?s=books&ie=UTF8&qid=1521489772&sr=1-2
3. https://www.kaggle.com/drscarlat/predict-hospital-length-of-stay-los-regression
4. https://www.kaggle.com/drscarlat/predict-hospital-length-of-stay-classification

10. Unsupervised Anomaly Detection in Antibiograms

While previous chapters have described supervised ML models of regression and classification, in this chapter we're going to detect anomalies in antibiotic resistance patterns using an unsupervised ML model.

By definition, anomalies are rare, unpredictable events so we usually don't have labeled samples of anomalies to train a supervised ML model. Even if we had labeled samples of anomalies - a supervised model will not be able to identify a new anomaly, one it has never seen during training. The true magic of unsupervised learning is the ML model capability to identify an anomaly never seen before.

The Python code and the dataset used for this chapter are available at Kaggle [1].

Data

The data for this chapter is based on a subset of MIMIC3 - Multiparameter Intelligent Monitoring in Intensive Care - a de-identified, freely available ICU database from Physionet [2].
Using SQL as detailed in my book [3], a dataset of 25,448 antibiograms was extracted. The initial dataset includes 140 unique microorganisms and their resistance / sensitivity
to 29 antibiotics arranged in 25.4k rows:

	Organism	Amikacin	Ampicillin	AMPICILLIN_SULBACTAM	CEFAZOLIN	CEFEPIME	CEFPODOXIME	CEFTAZIDIME	CEFTRIAXONE	CHLORAMP
0	STAPH AUREUS COAG +	0	0	0	0	0	0	0	0	0
1	ENTEROCOCCUS SP.	0	-1	0	0	0	0	0	0	0
2	KLEBSIELLA PNEUMONIAE	0	0	1	1	1	0	1	1	0
3	STAPH AUREUS COAG +	0	0	0	0	0	0	0	0	0
4	STREPTOCOCCUS MITIS	0	0	0	0	0	0	0	0	0
5	STAPH AUREUS COAG +	0	0	0	0	0	0	0	0	0
6	ENTEROCOCCUS SP.	0	-1	0	0	0	0	0	0	1
7	KLEBSIELLA PNEUMONIAE	0	0	1	1	1	0	1	1	0
	ENTEROCOCCUS									

- (+1) = organism is sensitive to antibiotic
- 0 = information not available
- (-1) = organism is resistant to antibiotic

Summarizing the above table by grouping on the organisms, produces a general antibiogram:

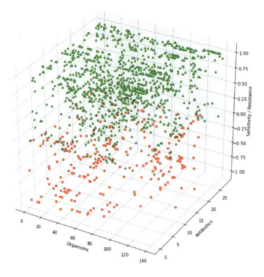

A view perpendicular to the Organisms axis on the above chart, becomes the projection of all the organisms and their relative sensitivity vs. resistance to all antibiotics:

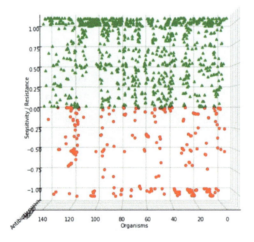

The view perpendicular to the Antibiotics axis becomes the projection of all the antibiotics and the relevant susceptibility of all the organisms:

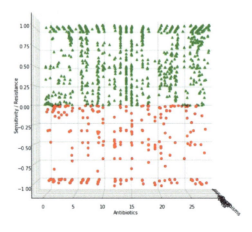

The challenge is to detect an anomaly that may manifest itself as a slight change of an organism susceptibility to one antibiotic, for example along the black dashed line in the diagram below. During testing of the ML model, we'll gradually modify one organism susceptibility to one antibiotic and test the model on F1 score, repeatedly, at different levels of susceptibility:

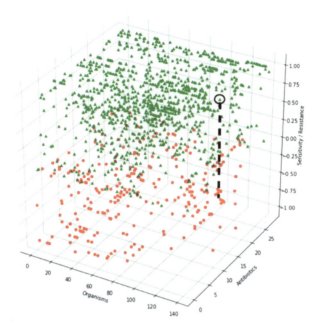

Let's focus on the most frequent organism in the data set - Staph Aureus Coag Positive (Staph). Staph has 6,925 samples out of 25.4k (27.2% of the whole dataset) and its average antibiogram in a projected 3D view:

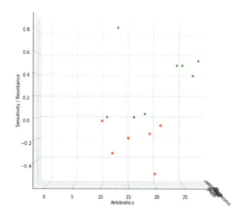

The above chart projected on 2D and rotated 90 degrees clockwise, depicts the average antibiogram of Staph:

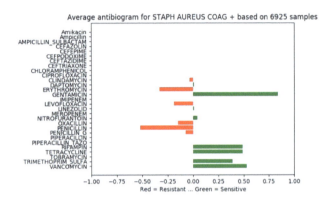

Note that in the above diagram, 0 has an additional meaning besides 'info n/a'. Zero may be also the result of averaging a number of sensitive with the same number of resistant samples and thus an average of zero susceptibility.

Model

Task: unsupervised anomaly detection in antibiograms, a binary decision: normal vs. anomaly
Experience: 25.4k antibiograms defined as normal for model training purposes
Performance: F1 score at various degrees of anomalies applied to the average antibiogram of one organism - Staph - and one antibiotic at a time

Local Outlier Factor (LOF) is an anomaly detection algorithm introduced in 2000, which finds outliers by comparing their location with respect to a given number of neighbors (k). LOF takes a local approach to better detect outliers about their neighbors, whereas other global strategies, might not be the best detection for datasets that fluctuate in density.

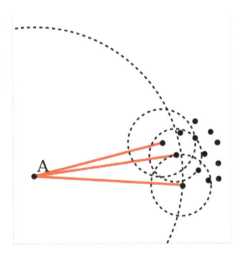

If k = 3, then the point A in the above diagram will be considered an outlier by LOF, as it is too far from its nearest 3 neighbors.
From Wikipedia [4].

A comparison of four outlier detection algorithm from scikit-learn - yellow dots are inliers and blue ones are outliers, with LOF in the right most column below:

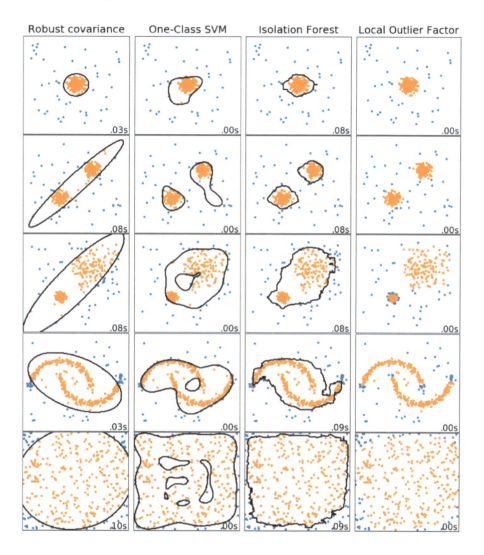

From Scikit-Learn [5].

The LOF model is initially trained with the original antibiograms dataset, which the model will memorize as normal.
After the model was trained, we gradually modify the Staph susceptibility to:

- Vancomycin only: from the original +0.5 to 0.4, 0.2, 0, -0.2,... -1.0
- Gentamicin only: from the original +0.8 to 0.4, 0.2, 0, -0.2,... -1.0
- Both antibiotics at the same time: 0.4, 0.2, 0, -0.2,... -1.0 sensitivity / resistance

Below is a Staph antibiogram with only 13% sensitive to Gentamicin - compared to the normal Staph antibiotic susceptibility at 83% for the same antibiotic:

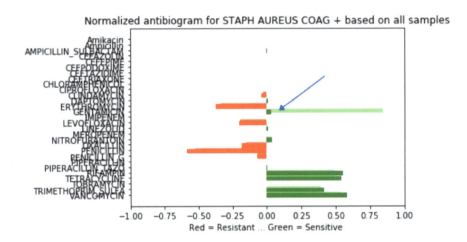

And the same comparison as above, but with a Staph population that is 13% resistant to Gentamicin:

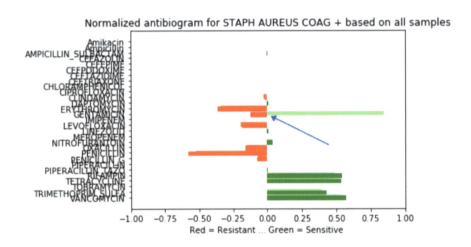

Performance

The last example, Staph susceptibility to Gentamicin significantly shifting from (+0.83) to (-0.13), creates a confusion matrix with the following performance metrics:

- Accuracy: 87.3%
- Recall: 82.6%
- Precision: 91.3%
- F1 score: 0.867

At each antibiotic sensitivity / resistance level applied as above, the model performance is measured with F1 score (the harmonic mean of precision and recall detailed in previous chapters). The model performance charted over a range of Staph susceptibilities to Vancomycin, Gentamicin and both antibiotics:

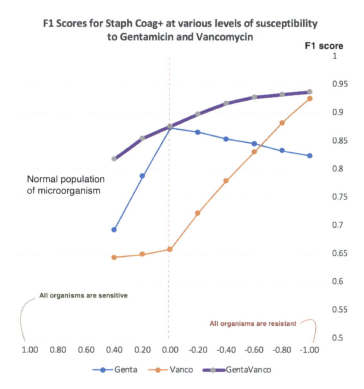

F1 Scores for Staph Coag+ at various levels of susceptibility to Gentamicin and Vancomycin

The more significant an anomaly of an antibiogram is, the higher the F1 score of the model.
An anomaly may manifest itself as a single large change in the sensitivity of one organism to one antibiotic, or as several small changes in the resistance to multiple antibiotics happening at the same time.
A chart of LOF model performance over a range of anomalies, can provide insights into the model capabilities at a specific F1 score. For example, at F1 = 0.75, Staph sensitivity to Gentamicin declining from (+0.83) to (+0.2) will be flagged as an anomaly, but the same organism changing its Vancomycin sensitivity from (+0.53) to (-0.2) will not be flagged as an anomaly.

There are no hard coded rules in the form of *if...then...* when using an unsupervised ML model. As there are no anomalies either, to use as labeled samples, there is a need to synthetically create outliers for testing the model performance, by modifying samples features in what (we believe) may simulate an anomaly.
In all the testing scenarios performed with the LOF model, these synthetic anomalies have always been in one direction: from an existing level of sensitivity towards a more resistant organism, as this is the direction the bacteria are developing under the evolutionary pressures of antibiotics. A microorganism developing a new sensitivity towards an antibiotic is practically unheard of, as it dooms the bacteria to commit suicide when exposed to an antibiotic to which it was previously resistant.

Unsupervised anomaly detection is a promising area of development in AI, as these ML models have shown their uncanny, magic capabilities to sift thru large datasets and decide under their own volition - what's normal and what should be considered an anomaly.

References:

1. https://www.kaggle.com/drscarlat/anomaly-detection-in-antibiograms-w-lof/edit
2. https://mimic.physionet.org/
3. book https://www.amazon.com/dp/1544093373/ref=sr_1_2?s=books&ie=UTF8&qid=1521489772&sr=1-2
4. https://en.wikipedia.org/wiki/Local_outlier_factor
5. https://scikit-learn.org/stable/modules/outlier_detection.html#outlier-detection

11. Basics of Computer Vision

The best ML models in computer vision, as measured by various image classification competitions, are the deep-learning, convolutional neural networks. A convolutional NN (convnet) for image analysis usually has an input layer, several hidden layers, and one output layer — like a regular, densely or fully connected NN, we've met already in previous chapters:

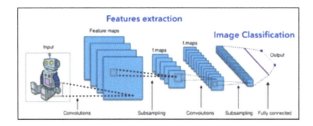

Modified from Wikipedia [1].

The input layer of a convnet will accept a tensor in the form of:

- Image height
- Image width
- Number of channels: one if gray scale and three if colored (red, green, blue)

What we see as the digit 8 in gray scale, the computer sees as a 28 x 28 x 1 tensor, representing the intensity of the black color (0 to 255) at a specific location of a pixel:

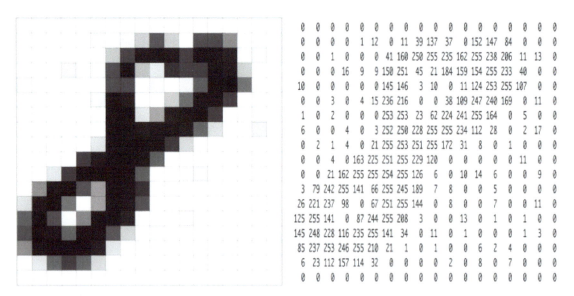

From Machine Learning is Fun [2].

A color image would have three channels (RGB) and the input tensor would be image height x width x 3.

A convnet has two main parts: one that extracts features from an image and another, usually made of several fully connected NN layers, that classifies the features extracted and predicts an output — the image class. What is different from a regular NN and what makes a convnet so efficient in tasks involving vision perception are the layers responsible for the features extraction:

- Convolutional layers that learn local patterns of increasingly complex shapes
- Subsampling layers that downsize the feature map created by the convolutional layers while maximizing the presence of various features

Convolutional Layer

A convolutional layer moves a filter over an input feature map and summarizes the results in an output feature map:

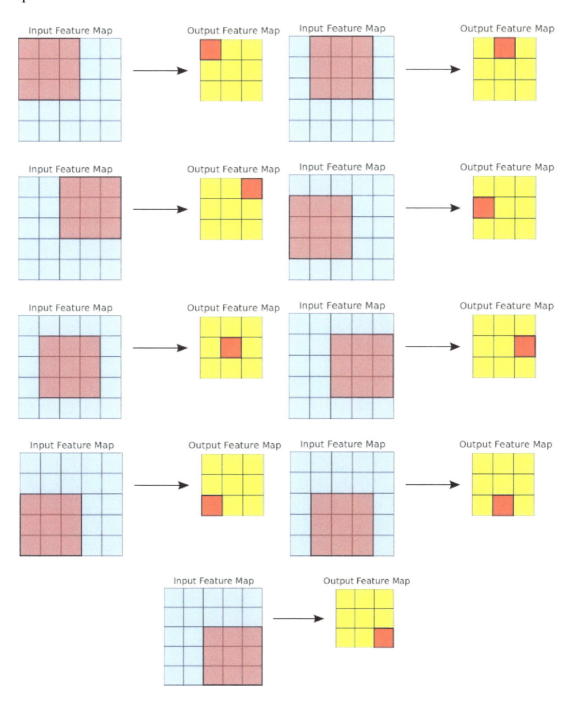

In the following example, the input feature map is a 5 x 5 x 1 tensor (which initially could have been the original image). The 3 x 3 convolutional filter is moved over the input feature map while creating the output feature map:

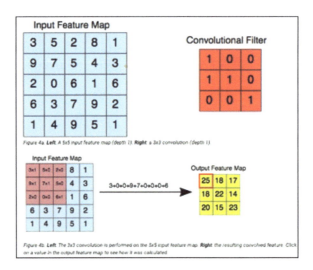

Subsampling Max Pool Layer

The input of the Max Pool subsampling layer is the output of the previous convolutional layer. Max pool layer output is a smaller tensor that maximizes the presence of certain learned features:

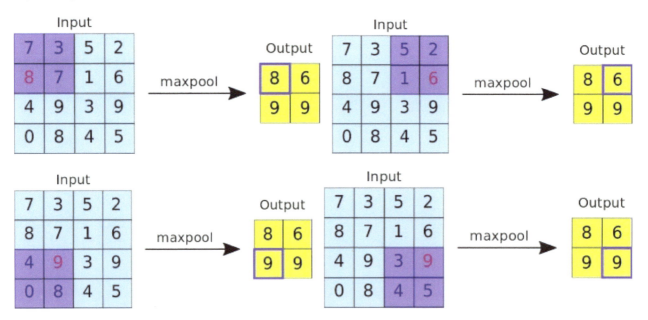

From ML Practicum: Image classification [3].

Filters and Feature Maps

Original image:

A simple 2 x 2 filter such as:

[+1,+1]
[-1, -1]

will detect horizontal lines in an image. The output feature map after applying the filter:

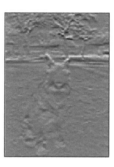

While a similar 2 x 2 filter:
[+1,-1]
[+1,-1]

will detect vertical lines in the same image, as the following output feature map shows:

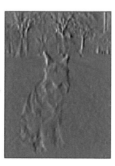

The filters of a convnet layer (like the simple filters used above for the horizontal and vertical line detection) are learned by the model during the training process. Here are the filters learned by a convnet first layer:

From Deep Learning Practitioners [4].

Local vs. Global Pattern Recognition

The main difference between a fully-connected NN we've met previously and a convnet, is that the fully connected NN learns global patterns, while a convnet learns local patterns in an image. This fact translates into the main advantages of a convnet over a regular NN with image analysis problems:

Spatial Hierarchy

The first, deepest convolutional layers detect basic shapes and colors: horizontal, vertical, oblique lines, green spots, etc. The next convolutional layers detect more complex shapes such as curved lines, rectangles, circles, ellipses while the next layers identify the shape, texture and color of ears, eyes, noses, etc. The last layers may learn to identify higher abstract features, such as cat vs. dog facial characteristics – that can help with the final image classification.

A convnet learns during the training phase the spatial hierarchy of local patterns in an image:

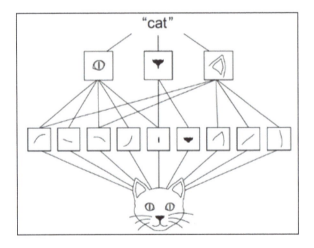

From Deep Learning with Python [5].

Translation and Position Invariant

A convnet will identify a circle in the left lower corner of an image, even if during training the model was exposed only to circles appearing in the right upper corner of the images. Object or shape location within an image, zoom, angle, shear, etc. have almost no effect on a convnet capability to extract features from an image.

In contrast, a fully-connected, dense NN will need to be trained on a sample for each possible object location, position, zoom, angle, etc. as it learns only global patterns from an image. A regular NN will require an extremely large number of (only slightly different) images for training. A convnet is more data efficient than a NN, as it needs a smaller number of samples to learn local patterns and features that in turn have more generalization power.

The two filters below and their output feature maps — identifying oblique lines in an image. The convnet is invariant to the actual line position within the image. It will identify a local pattern disregarding its global location:

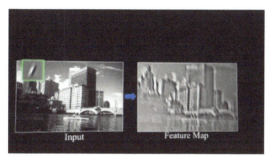 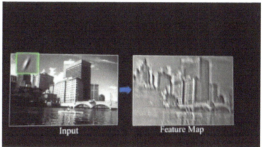

From Intuitive Explanation of Convnets [6].

Transfer Learning

Training a convnet on millions of labeled images necessitates powerful computers to work in parallel for many days and weeks. That's usually cost prohibitive for most of us. Instead, one can use a pre-trained computer vision model that is available as open source.

Keras (an open source ML framework) offers 10 such image analysis, pre-trained models. All these models have been trained and tested on standard ImageNet databases. Their top, last layer has the same 1,000 categories: dogs, cats, planes, cars, etc. as this was the standardized challenge for the model.

There are two main methods to perform a transfer learning and use this amazing wealth of image analysis experience accumulated by these pre-trained models:

Feature Extraction

- Import a pre-trained model such as VGG16 without the top layer. The 1,000 categories of ImageNet standard challenge are most probably not well aligned with your goals.
- Freeze the imported model so it will not be modified during training.
- Add on top of the imported model, your own NN — usually a fully-connected, dense NN — that is trainable.

Fine Tuning

- Import a pre-trained model without the top layer,
- Freeze the model so it will not be modified during training, except …
- Unfreeze the last block of layers of the imported model, so this block will be trainable.
- Add on top of the imported model, your own NN, usually a dense NN.
- Train the ML model with a slow learning rate. Large modifications to the original pre-trained model weights of its last block will practically destroy their "knowledge."

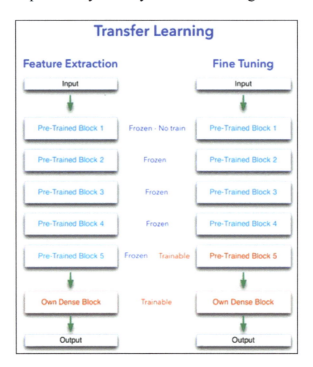

References:

1. https://de.wikipedia.org/wiki/Convolutional_Neural_Network
2. https://medium.com/@ageitgey/machine-learning-is-fun-part-3-deep-learning-and-convolutional-neural-networks-f40359318721
3. https://developers.google.com/machine-learning/practica/image-classification/convolutional-neural-networks
4. https://www.amazon.com/Deep-Learning-Practitioners-Josh-Patterson/dp/1491914254
5. https://www.amazon.com/Deep-Learning-Python-Francois-Chollet/dp/1617294438
6. https://ujjwalkarn.me/2016/08/11/intuitive-explanation-convnets/

12. Identify Melanoma in Images

In this last chapter, we'll train a ML model to diagnose melanoma in dermoscopic images. The original data is the HAM10k images dataset, Human Against Machine with 10,000 Training Images [1], which is freely available [2].

The dermoscopic images in the HAM10k dataset have been curated and normalized in terms of luminosity, colors, resolution, etc. The actual diagnosis was validated by histopathology (a.k.a. source of truth) in more than 50 percent of the cases, which is twice more than the previously available skin lesion datasets. The rest of the lesions' diagnosis was based on a consensus of dermatologists. The 10k images in this dataset belong to the following seven diagnostic categories:

Actinic Keratoses – 327 images solar keratoses, intraepithelial carcinoma, Bowen's disease (akiec)

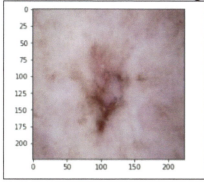

Basal Cell Carcinoma – 514 images (bcc)

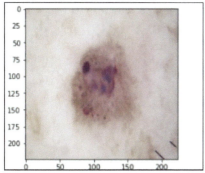

Benign Keratosis – 1,099 images seborrheic keratoses, senile wart, solar lentigo, lichen-planus like keratosis (bkl)

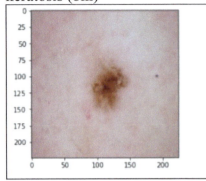

Dermatofibroma – 115 images (df)

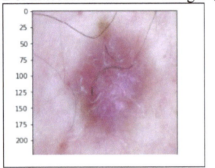

Melanocytic Nevus – 6,705 images (nv)

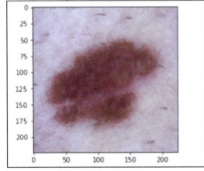

Melanoma – 1,113 images (mel)

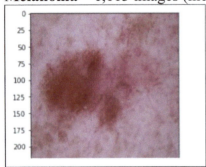

Vascular Lesions – 142 images cherry angiomas, angiokeratomas, and pyogenic granulomas (vasc)

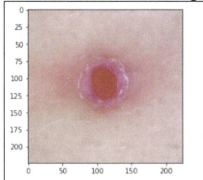

The dataset is imbalanced, as the number of images in each class varies from 115 (dermatofibroma) to 6,705 (nevus):

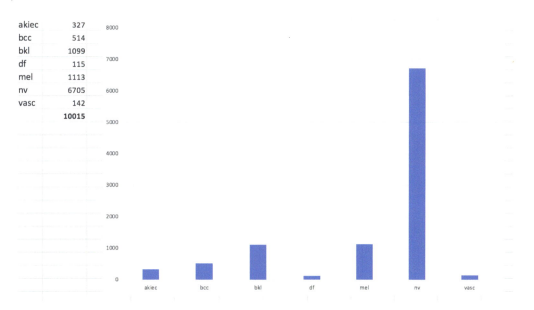

akiec	327
bcc	514
bkl	1099
df	115
mel	1113
nv	6705
vasc	142
	10015

Instead of trying to classify seven skin lesions with a highly imbalanced dataset, let's simplify the task to the diagnosis of Melanoma vs. Not Melanoma. If we summarize the above categories into two groups, the result is still an imbalanced dataset with:

- 1,113 Melanoma images
- 8,902 Not Melanoma

We can apply data augmentation to the Melanoma group and bring the number of images to be similar to the Not Melanoma group. Data augmentation applies a random combination of image modifications — such as zoom, angle, shift, horizontal and vertical flips, etc. — and creates synthetic images.

Original image of melanoma

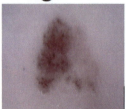

Synthetically created images of melanoma

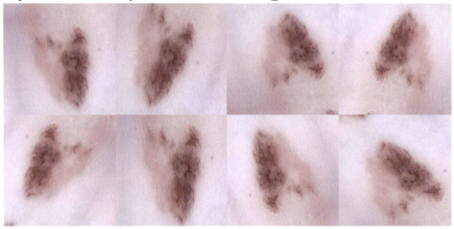

Data augmentation allows the model to be exposed to various modifications of an image of melanoma. This in turn allows the model to learn and later generalize, for example, that a melanoma pointing to the left is still a melanoma if it points to the right. The previously imbalanced 10k images become a 17.8k balanced dataset after the data augmentation of the melanoma group:

- 8,903 Melanoma images
- 8,902 Not Melanoma images

With such a balanced dataset, the guessing accuracy should be 50 percent. This is the baseline sanity check before we measure a machine performance on this binary classification task.

Melanoma or Not Melanoma

Task: categorize a dermoscopic image as Melanoma or Not melanoma, a supervised binary classification challenge
Experience: the 17.8k dermoscopic images dataset detailed above
Performance: accuracy, precision, recall, F1 score, and ROC AUC

The newly created 17.8k images dataset is randomly split into three datasets:

- Train 10,682 images (60 percent)
- Validate 3,562 (20 percent)
- Test 3,561 (20 percent)

This image analysis challenge is approached from three angles, as explained in the last chapter:

1. Create a convolutional NN (convnet) from scratch
2. Use existing pre-trained models for feature extraction
3. Fine tune existing pre-trained models

Common to all the following convolutional NN models:

- Input layer that accepts an image as a tensor: image height (pixels) x width x color (RGB). The models tested accept images from 224x224x3 to 331x331x3.
- Output layer that predicts a probability between 0 and 1 for the image being Melanoma vs. Not Melanoma. The decision cutoff point is 0.5.
- In between the above two layers, various architectures of convolutional, pooling, dense, and normalization layers, with millions of trainable parameters (a.k.a. neurons)

Simple Convolutional NN

The Python code and the dataset for this part are publicly available [3].

This convnet, with 9.7M trainable parameters, achieves an accuracy of 93 percent on the test dataset of images the model has never seen. The learning curves for 100 training epochs of this model, while using dropout, regularizers, and batch normalization techniques:

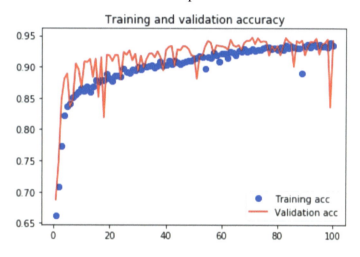

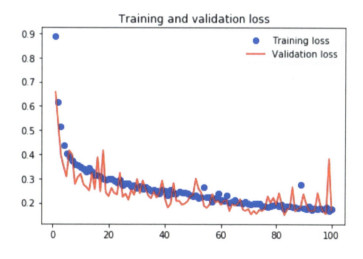

Transfer Learning

Feature extraction and fine-tuning are two common methods of transfer learning. For the following transfer learning, I've cross-validated eight open source, pre-trained image analysis models: VGG16, VGG19, ResNet50, InceptionResNetV2, Xception, InceptionV3, DenseNet201, and NasNetLarge. All these computer vision models are freely available as part of Keras, the ML framework used for this image analysis project [4].

Feature Extraction

As explained in the last article, with feature extraction, we import one of the above models and freeze it so it won't be modified during the training process and we add our own trainable layers on top of this pre-trained model. The lowest accuracy results: 86.3 percent with feature extraction on top of VGG16. The highest accuracy was achieved with a model extracting features from ResNet50, 94.5 percent. Note that after 50 epochs, this model was still underfitting on accuracy while perfectly fitting the loss function:

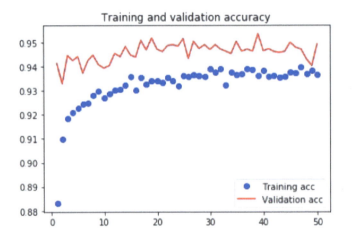

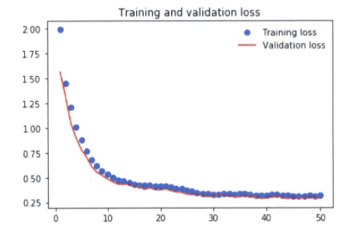

The Python notebook and the data for the feature extraction (ResNet50) are available at [5].

Fine Tuning

Fine tuning is slightly different that feature extraction. While we still import a pre-trained model and freeze it, we unfreeze the model last block of layers so these block weights will be modified during training. Fine tuning is usually done with a slow learning rate since we do not want to modify the pre-learned weights of the model last block too abruptly, as this may destroy the units (a.k.a. neurons) pre-learned "knowledge."

The worst performance with fine tuning a pre-trained model was 92 percent – NasNetLarge.

The best overall performance on this dataset – **94.7 percent accuracy** – was achieved by fine tuning ResNet50, the same pre-trained model introduced above. This time the model has 10.8M trainable parameters and it displays the following learning curves:

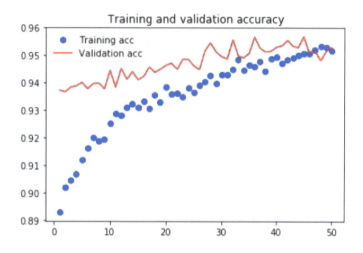

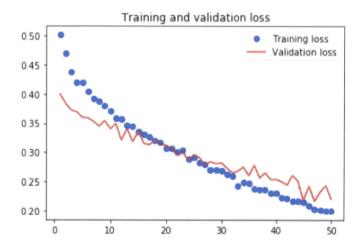

The Python notebook and the images dataset are available at [6].

Model Performance Evaluation

As previously mentioned, there are other metrics besides accuracy that convey information on the relevance of the results:

- Confusion matrix (TP,TN, FP and FN)
- Precision
- Recall
- F1 score
- ROC AUC

Considering only the best model in terms of accuracy, fine tuning on top of a pre-trained ResNet50:

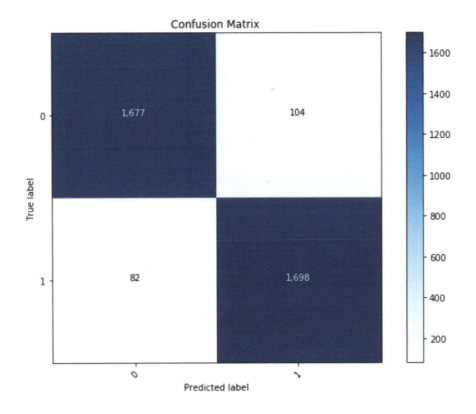

This confusion matrix translates into:

- TN: 1677
- FP: 104
- FN: 82
- TP: 1698

Final metrics for the best ML model:
- Accuracy: 94.8 percent
- Recall: 95.4 percent
- Precision: 94.2 percent
- F1Score: 0.948
- ROC AUC: 0.947

Performance Comparison on Similar Melanoma Identification Tasks

Dermatologist ROC AUC performance varies between 0.69 [7] and 0.91 [8].
Other ML models ROC AUC performance varies between 0.72 [9] and 0.94 [10].

Conclusions

- Using freely available infrastructure, framework, Python libraries, and a single dataset, one can build a ML model that outperforms both dermatologists and other ML models in the detection of melanoma in dermoscopic images.
- By definition, a learning algorithm will improve its performance on a specific task with each and every new experience learned, so the above algorithm is expected to improve beyond **94.8** percent accuracy if it will be exposed to additional relevant images.
- A fully operational ML model would have to predict in real time each new image it sees, whether it is melanoma or not, with the probability of the decision. Such a ML model will need to fine tune itself, on a daily or weekly basis, by being re-trained on newly labeled images, those with the ground truth reached by consensus or histopathology results. The periodical retraining of the ML model is analogous to the continued medical education of any healthcare professional.
- A reportedly shortage of dermatologists in the US, combined with the introduction of full-body 3D photography that produces hundreds and thousands of images per patient, may hint towards the future of this type of ML models — not replacing dermatologists, but supporting them with the pre-screening process of the millions of images coming their way.

References:

1. https://www.nature.com/articles/sdata2018161
2. https://dataverse.harvard.edu/dataset.xhtml?persistentId=doi:10.7910/DVN/DBW86T
3. https://www.kaggle.com/drscarlat/melanoma-my-own-convnet
4. https://keras.io/applications/

Epilogue

I hope this book has clarified the main terms and concepts in AI, demystified some buzzwords, and in the process, has left you with some wisdom and curiosity about ML.

As I am always curious about new ideas in AI/ML in healthcare, please let me know about *your* interesting machine intelligence challenges.

Index

computer vision · 6, 85
confusion matrix · 68
consolidate · 25
consultations · 8
context · 33
continuous · 11
continuous variable · 10
contour chart · 15
control · 50
convnet · 85
convoluted · 44
convolutional · 85
Convolutional Layer · 86
cost function · 22
CPT · 30
creatinine · 34
cross-evaluated · 71
cross-validation · 54
Curse of Dimensionality · 31

D

daily average · 59
Data Augmentation · 57, 94
dataset · 38
decision boundary · 17
decision making process · 65
deep-learning · 85
dermatologists · 8, 92
dermoscopic · 92
deterioration · 29
diagnosis · 8
dictionary · 31
differential diagnosis · 6
Digital assistants · 6
dimension · 16
dimensionality · 31
discrete · 16
distance · 36
distribution · 27
diverse · 25
dogs and cats · 57
DRG · 30
Dropout · 58

E

elliptical · 28
ensemble · 8
entity · 35
epoch · 36
error · 19
estimate · 69
ethnicity · 30
evolutionary pressures · 84
experience · 7, 12
expression · 21

F

G

H

I

ABOUT THE AUTHOR

I am a physician and data scientist, board-certified in anesthesiology with a degree in computer sciences. I have a keen interest in machine intelligence applications in healthcare - https://scarlatsquared.wordpress.com/ .

This is my third book - the previous ones dealt with the structured systems analysis of the EHR and SQL applied to medical databases.

I welcome your feedback on this book at drscarlat [at] gmail.com

Some Kind Reviews

Machine learning is becoming more important in healthcare, and those in clinical informatics are at the forefront. Unfortunately, the complexity of the topic precludes most physicians from learning it. The content in Scarlat ML Primer for Clinicians, taken slowly and in order, is designed at the perfect level for clinicians. It allows one to understand the basics and facilitate further discussions and practical implementations.
Rod Tarrago MD
CMIO, Seattle Children's Hospital, USA

Who doesn't write, comment and talk about machine learning, artificial intelligence, block-chain etc. nowadays? Dr. Scarlat has taken upon himself one of the most complex aspects of what and how we learn as physicians: a smooth transition from theory into practice. I admit feeling a surge of endorphins while reading "How Does a Machine Actually Learn?". Pure intellectual bliss. Without doubts, my knowledge on AI increased while reading his book. Read it yourself and it will satisfy your curiosity and even hunger about AI and the amazing uses in medicine.
Bernardo Andrés Perez MD
Chief Scientific Officer Wellian & Hospital General de Granollers, Spain

Are you confused by all the terms surrounding machine learning, artificial intelligence or deep learning? Want to understand these new technology and how it applies to the world of healthcare and what it can and cannot do? This book offers a great introduction, through the eyes of a physician on the innovations possible and how to achieve them with these new tools. Learn how this technology will change the way we practice medicine and deliver healthcare and teach you how to be part of this new world and how to use these tools and even develop and program your own models.
Nick van Terheyden, MD
CEO – Incremental Health, USA

It's easy to generate buzz around the promise of data to drive medical decision making. Unfortunately, concept and reality can be two very different things, and it's impossible to develop an informed opinion, let alone take action, without an understanding of the actual potential. Dr. Scarlat manages to pull off two feats at once: On the practical side, he teaches readers immediately useful skills via step-by-step breakdown of specific projects. At the same time, his walkthroughs pull back the curtain and demystify the world of how medical data is organized, accessed, and can be analyzed. Dr. Scarlat gives readers everything needed to create their own vision of what's possible along with the ability to get started themselves in the new domain of machine intelligence in healthcare.
Chris Schlanger MD
Mercy Hospital & Virtual Care development, USA

Simply outstanding and easy to understand. comprehensively outline the difference between traditional healthcare practice and the impact of ML and technology on future of the medicine.
Avnish Rastogi
Microsoft Azure Cloud, USA